Worth Noting

# Worth Noting

## *Editorials, Letters, Essays, an Interview and Bibliography*

SANFORD BERMAN

*Foreword by* BILL KATZ

McFarland & Company, Inc., Publishers
*Jefferson, North Carolina, and London*

*The present work is a reprint of the library bound edition of*
Worth Noting : Editorials, Letters, Essays, an Interview, and
Bibliography, *first published in 1988 by McFarland.*

ALTERNATIVE CATALOGUING-IN-PUBLICATION DATA

Berman, Sanford, 1933–
    Worth noting : editorials, letters, essays, an interview, and
bibliography / Sanford Berman ; foreword by Bill Katz.
        p.    cm.

    ISBN 978-0-7864-9351-7
    softcover : acid free paper

    Partial contents: Cataloging.—Censorship/human
rights.—Creationism.
    1. Cataloging.   2. Censorship.   3. Human right.
    4. Librarians—Social responsibility.   5. Creationism.
    I. Title.   II. Katz, Bill, 1924– Foreword.

LIBRARY OF CONGRESS CATALOGUING-IN-PUBLICATION DATA

Berman, Sanford, 1933–
    Worth noting : editorials, letters, essays, an interview, and
bibliography / Sanford Berman ; foreword by Bill Katz.
        p.    cm.
    Includes bibliographical references and index.

    ISBN 978-0-7864-9351-7
    softcover : acid free paper ∞

    1. Library science.   2. Cataloging.   3. Censorship.
    4. Creationism.   I. Title.
    Z674.B44 2014        081        87–43165

BRITISH LIBRARY CATALOGUING DATA ARE AVAILABLE

Front cover image (iStockphoto/Thinkstock)

Manufactured in the United States of America

*McFarland & Company, Inc., Publishers*
    *Box 611, Jefferson, North Carolina 28640*
    *www.mcfarlandpub.com*

# CONTENTS

# FOREWORD

## BY BILL KATZ

In a world longing for heroes, let's pay tribute to Sandy Berman, a librarian and an affectionate hero of an unusual order. Right off, there's a problem. How can one write a tribute to read as more than an early obituary. A sense of proportion indicates that no one, not even the hero, is perfect. For all we know Sandy has dark thoughts of giving up books for computers, of turning from cataloging to administration. Still, we must deal with what is offered, not what is threatened.

The life of the man from Hennepin County has the resonance of the heroes in Raymond Carver's short stories, or the individuals who people Sherwood Anderson's America. There is such a close integration of style and sincerity in Sandy's life and his work that he is a modern day eccentric who, without the slightest hesitation, refuses to be anyone but himself. Who is the persona? The quickest way to discover the answer is to turn to his writings, and more particularly this collection. If anything characterizes his work it is high ideals.

The difficulty is that high ideals rarely make for high drama. Sandy may well be the exception. He takes on the outside world with such vigor that his sense of outrage, often tempered with satire and wit, gives anyone with a sense of the ridiculous (and the sublime) pause. There may be more to America than Colonel North, and considerably more to librarianship than the American Library Association and the Library of Congress. Perhaps Sandy's greatest contribution to library literature is that his writing is truly lucid. It may be good causes that drive him on, but what makes him convincing is his fortunate method of presentation, his ability to document his concerns with lively examples—see, e.g., his attack on the tortured syntax and countless neologisms of card catalog headings. One finds oneself involuntarily smiling at this volatile, quick witted concern about subject headings. Just for the pleasure of studying the lack of sensibility of bureaucrats, he is not to be missed. Sandy's books, essays and correspondence add up to a one man information service. His letters, usually entertaining trouble for those who fail to respond to pleas for a cause, are famous among friends and foes. Hardly a week or so goes by that the familiar envelope from Hennepin County does not appear filled with this or that group of clippings, notes and observations on everything from the latest cataloging rule to an outrageous censorship decision. Anyone who needs a pen pal should turn to the man from Hennepin County. There is no end to the wealth, the presentation of material which Sandy makes available. In the field of correspondence alone he has no rival in the library profession.

Heroes, even the more modest type, need a certain degree of hostility. Their irritating complaints would be pointless without the reassurance of the opposites whose material interests are challenged. The foes' numerical superiority is nothing. Sandy is willing to do battle with the Library of Congress as well as with uncomprehending philistines in any library slot. He fears and mistrusts only the complacent. The amount of work he has produced indicates his efforts are not unappreciated, particularly by foes whose uninterrupted insipidity he challenges.

There is no hero without doubt and Sandy comes to question even himself from time to time. For example, see his modification of an earlier position as a "100% First Amendment purist" in the reprinted interview "Alternative Perspectives." One can admire, if not entirely agree with, a man who remains less than blind to the merits of a long standing position.

There is no argument with Sandy's other positions. See, for example, the section on Human Rights in this collection. Here the causes are as realistic as the observations on their importance to the library world. Here the writer surpasses himself, arousing anger in the reader over the gallery of wrongs. Here, too, are solutions which earnestly call on us all to be heroes of sorts.

The extracts from the continuing war with creationism gives one hope that the world is not entirely governed by well meaning fools. The only indiscretions here are ones of intellectual delight over the sometimes truly zany and self-satisfied arguments of the sheep in the field of creationism and other forms of what Sandy calls "that old time religion."

When one turns to the select bibliography, one may first think that the author is, in fact, a one man literary academy endowed with the energy and skill of not one, but ten or more writers. Every reader will have a favorite essay, passage or eye-witness record of emphatic foolishness, but for starts try the "Terrible truth about teenlit cataloging." No wonder so many kids so meticulously turn from books to MTV.

Does all of this add up to a profile of a hero? If one believes in the joys of enlightening battle, then the answer is a resounding yes. But we have come to praise, not to bury. With luck and care, the hero and his numerous efforts will go on to assure that we share the critical judgment and humanity which makes librarianship a conspicuous delight.

# CATALOGING

# *HERRENVOLK* LANGUAGE

Out of the South African milieu, and as a footnote to previous remarks on the continued use of pejorative, defamatory nomenclature in subject-heading schemes, "scholarly" tomes, periodicals, and ordinary speech: Andre Brink, lecturer at Rhodes University and Afrikaans-speaking poet-novelist-playwright, has lately declared

> This may seem trivial. But I have become increasingly aware of a tendency among Afrikaans "highbrows" to refer to Africans as "Kaffers." [The term appears as "Kafirs" in the U.S. Library of Congress subject-heading list, 7th ed., p. 697.] A decade or so ago it was done universally, and not always with disrespect. Then the Establishment enforced the use of "Bantu" ["Bantus" in the LC-list, p. 112]. Now it seems to become the vogue again to prove how "verlig" one can be by saying "Kaffer" again. *The simple point is that any word like Kaffer, Bantoe, etc., is a denial of the human individuality of another person* (as American soldiers talk of Gooks and Viets — until they can massacre women and children). It should be a simple but remarkably effective remedy to consciously propagate the use of the words "man," "woman" and "child" for anybody in this country, irrespective of colour. In situations where, for some reason, it is absolutely imperative to distinguish colour (and I think one will discover that there are surprisingly few such situations), it should be easy to refer to a black man or a white woman or a brown child. I have said that this seems trivial. *But a word is a symptom of an entire attitude; and perhaps one can eventually change attitudes by simply starting with elementary words respecting the humanity of people.*

See "Some aspects of culture and Apartheid," in Study Project on Christianity in Apartheid Society, *Anatomy of Apartheid* (Johannesburg, Spro-Cas, 1970), page 42. Emphases added.

Brink's observations may serve as a preface to as well as partial (albeit accidental) comment on, the following statement submitted by Dr. Mallory Wober, who lectures in sociology at Makerere University (Kampala, Uganda):

> *re: Pygmies.* One does better to look in an etymological dictionary to learn

*Reprinted from* MISR Library Accessions List/Bulletin, *December 1971, pp. 18–20.*

about this word. It comes from a Greek word *pugmi,* meaning fist, then referring to the length of measure from the elbow to the knuckles. The word is
essentially similar to "cubit." It was applied to people told about in the non-
usually-verifiable stories of the occasional distant travellers from whom the
Greeks knew anything about Central Africa. Maybe these were thought to
be as small as a fore-arm length, maybe it meant "elbow-high" people. There
is nothing pejorative about the term, and it applies strictly to stature. Any
reference to pejorative content, in the O.E.D. [i.e., *Oxford English dictionary*],
is metaphorically added on, and there is no means of telling—apart from a
survey—whether many or most people find anything pejorative about the
term. The word incidentally relates to pugnacious, pugilist, peak, pike, and
others.

Maina-wa-Kinyatti's other remarks [quoted in the November 1971
bulletin, pp. 12–13] are also peculiar. "Native" is not a racist word; if we
remove it, there is a gap left in our semantically needful space which would
have to be filled by some other word. Bantu is perhaps a racist word in South
Africa, but it is not an invention of whites, and the thing they have adapted
it for is not to divide Africans, but to lump them together, in a way to unite
them conceptually, as a single entity. Negro is qualitatively no different
from Black, unless one prefers Anglo-Saxon to Latin roots. The fact that
neither of them are in my opinion correct, since hardly any people are actually Black (whom I have met or seen) but dark brown, perhaps does relate
to the words being used pejoratively. But it does not augur well for the aura
that may become attached to the word Black, if we assume that distance
from the actual truth enables people to invest words with meaning other
than that which, in this case, meets the eye. Kaffir is an Arabic word, meaning outsider, foreigner, and again tends to refer to an out-group as a bloc,
rather than to divide "the African race." As to pygmy, I don't see that we
*know* that white racists made this word; it was more likely to have arisen in
converse between Greek-speaking and other inhabitants of ancient Egypt,
about whose colour we can not be at all certain.

I don't think that emotional statements with but shaky foundations in
truth are any more helpful from Maina-wa-Kinyatti than when from A.R.
Jensen. If we oppose misconceptions foisted upon the public by the latter,
we should oppose them from the former. Doubtless Maina-wa-Kinyatti
writes out of a sincere motive to act so as to raise the self- and social esteem
of his people. Equally sincerely, I doubt whether this cause will be served
by false claims; they may even be "counter-productive."

Employing Dr. Wober's contribution as a springboard for further discussion: There appear to be two principal aspects to the problem of
nomenclature. One might be termed the dimension or imperative of intellectual honesty and scholarly accuracy, while the other revolves about the socio-
political import of names, embracing questions of ethics, effects, and human
justice. Sometimes, of course, the two intertwine or overlap. As Maina-wa-

Kinyatti noted, no African people calls *itself* "Pygmies." Nor has any group denoted *itself* "Kaffirs," "Bushmen," "Hottentots," or "Janjero." To leave the African context for a moment, it is common knowledge that Jews have been opprobriously labelled "Kikes" or "Judsau," Italians "wops," Asians (as Brink aptly mentions) "gooks" or "slopes," Germans "krauts," Americans "gringos," etc. While the ethnic group or nationality so named can be easily identified, no fair-minded person would argue that such defamatory rubrics merit general employment simply because of utility. All the cited examples — and the list could be extended indefinitely — function to underpin often malicious stereotypes, to de-humanize the subjects, transforming them into unsavory or at least worthless *objects*. Following Brink's insight, a word may, indeed, be "a symptom of an entire attitude." It is much easier to oppress "Kaffirs" rather than "Xhosas," to napalm "Gooks" instead of "Vietnamese," to ghettoize and degrade "Kikes," to wage holy war against "Pagans," to hang Zimbabwean or Namibian "terrorists," to exploit if not eradicate sub-human "natives" and "primitives" (with whom popular mythology conveniently equates cannibalism, infantility, and a host of other unlovely attributes). An etymological dictionary can well demonstrate that "Pygmies," e.g., *first* arose as merely a descriptive, non-pejorative term, or that "Negro" is the apparently innocent Iberian word for "black." Such data are surely interesting, but also insufficient. For what is crucial here is less the static *origin* than the subsequent, actual, dynamic *usage,* a word's emotive quality. On this plane, sources like the O.E.D., Webster's, and the affected parties themselves are altogether material. It can be amply shown that neither Africans nor other people of African descent, most notably Afro-Americans, appreciate being called "Negroes." To the linguistic purist this may seem a trifle, for he knows that etymologically Negroes = black = Negroes. Yet "Negro" *is* "qualitatively . . . different" from "black" (or the multiple "Afro-" forms). In its Latinized manifestation, it is irreversibly linked with the Hispano-Lusitanian slavers who regarded the Africans they ripped from their homeland as "a vile, immoral race possessing unclean blood and low intelligence." In America particularly its general use has shorn blacks there of their very identity, denying them a specific connection with "land, history and culture," all "factors" — according to one Afro-American spokesman — "which proclaim the humanity of an individual." Dr. Wober's opinion on the mutual inaccuracy of both "Negro" and "Black" is well-taken. In fact, many "Negroes" are not strictly, chromatically "black," while there *are* "blacks" — numbering in the millions — who are distinctly *not* of African descent (e.g., the widely-dispersed peoples of Southern India and Ceylon, as well as the indigenous Australians). To lump these latter peoples generically and ethnically with Africans and their kin of the diaspora would hardly promote clarity nor accuracy. Still, admitting the clumsiness and inaccuracy of "Blacks" as an across-the-board term does not therefore compel nor endorse the continued use of "Negroes." Once its essentially pejorative nature, together with its inefficacy as a typological/

descriptive label, are recognized, it can be painlessly discarded in favor of "Africans," "Afro-Americans," "Afro-Brazilians," "Afro-Guyanans," etc. There are plentiful precedents for so doing in scholarly literature and elsewhere.

In the specific case of "Kaffir," the word's etymology is unusually instructive. It stems, as Dr. Wober rightly says, from an Arabic root, but meant not only "outsider" or "foreigner," but also the more negatively-charged "unbeliever" or "infidel." It may certainly be argued that the term's employment in South Africa "refers to an out-group as a bloc" and thus should not be construed as a classic "divide-and-conquer" technique. Perhaps. Although within the context of South Africa's "plural" society, it may nicely function to further "divide" African, Asian, "Coloured," and White. There can be little argument, however, with the overriding fact that it is a palpably racist, disparaging rubric consciously employed to buttress *Herrenvolkism*. A 1969 UNESCO Meeting of Experts on Educational Methods Designed to Combat Racial Prejudice equated the word with "nigger." And it has been unequivocally denounced as offensive and totally unacceptable by — among others — the librarian at the University of Malawi, the South African Institute of Race Relations, the South African ANC, and Andre Brink (himself an Afrikaner). In short, while Maina-wa-Kinyatti's functional explanation may bear refinement, his damnation of the word as a racist, dehumanizing epithet appears well-founded.

It would be comfortable to agree that "Native" is "not a racist word," but a whole host of authorities emphatically *dis*agree. Fifteen years ago, Edward F. Dozier, an anthropologist, declared that

> The problem of terminological designation for nonliterate societies is an especially serious one. The fact that "primitive," "native," and similar terms are often placed in quotation marks indicates the shaky and unsure ground upon which they rest as designations for the societies which anthropologists study. That these terms are not used in a definitive and precise fashion reflects the growing and changing science of anthropology and also a changing world situation. As a science grows and matures it revises and regulates its terminology. More appropriate terms, in both a descriptive and taxonomic sense, replace the older and less appropriate designations. Among anthropologists there is an increasing awareness that these terms are unsatisfactory and inadequate.

Even earlier, social scientists like Herskovits and Mead (whom Dozier quotes) had rejected the value-laden terminology exemplified by "primitive" and "native" as "tendentious" and likely to antagonize the very peoples so described. More recently, A. Babs Fafunwa, the Nigerian educator, emphasized at the UNESCO Meeting of Experts that "native" has become endowed with notions of childlike simplicity and "non–European origin," and that "in terms of current usage is synonymous with the African." In a survey conducted among her students, an Afro-American high school teacher lately determined that "native" overwhelmingly produced associations with "cannibal," "African," "savage," etc. Abolishing "native" from standard nomenclature would indisputably leave a "gap . . . in our semantically needful space." But such gaps can surely be filled in both a humane and workable fashion.

Similarly with "Pygmy." It might be impossible to document that "racists" or "chauvinists" deliberately manufactured the word. Nevertheless, most literate persons—who have at some juncture read or seen phrases like "intellectual pygmy" or "moral pygmy"—understand at once the over- and under-tones it conveys. And they are obviously *negative*. Even as a "scientific" designation, the word slights and obscures the people it ostensibly names. To focus on the "Pygmies'" stature in our own nomenclature discloses much more about *us* than about *them*. It reveals a circus-side-show obsession with size and exotica, not a sympathetic interest in nor respect for the Mbuti, Twa, and others as *human beings*. The fact of their comparative shortness is a relatively superficial thing, certainly no sound basis for an *ethnic* or *cultural* classification. As a visually distinguishing feature—like color in other places—it may influence their social relationship with neighboring groups, etc., yet is not necessarily a signal determinant of their *internal* social structure and cultural patterns. Some equivalent of "Pygmies" may be justified as a biotaxonomic designation—though there doesn't appear to be a correlative term for tall-statured people (Ambrose Bierce once facetiously suggested "Hogmies")—but whether *any* single socio-cultural rubric should be applied to these groups, who inhabit not only portions of the Zaire Republic but also Rwanda and Zambia, as well as the Andaman Islands, Philippines, Malay Peninsula, and New Guinea, and who are *all* often interchangeably dubbed "Pygmies," "Dwarfs," "Negritos," or "Negrillos" (the latter two diminutives of "Negroes") solely on the size-plus-"woolly-hair"-criterion, regardless of habitat or ethnic traits, remains questionable. Expert opinion on this score would be most welcome.

Two operative principles may be tentatively posed from this exchange: 1. That people ought to be called by their *own* names, as far as this can be determined, rather than assigned the frequently-denigratory labels imposed by outsiders (e.g., the evidence demands substitution of *Khoi-Khoin* for the Boer-applied, manifestly derisive "Hottentots"); and 2. Demonstrably erroneous and/or offensive nomenclature like "Negroes," "primitive," "tribe," and "native" should be either abandoned or—if necessary—replaced by objectively accurate and wholly non-defamatory forms. Professor Peter Rigby, head of Makerere's sociology department, writing in the June 1971 *Mawazo*, claims that "the annoying use of such useless labels [as "primitive," "tribe," "pagan," etc.] in social science writing is gradually dying away, and the fatal thrusts against them have long since been delivered." "Dying away," possibly, in most social science literature (although the March 1971 edition of *Forthcoming books* cites five *new* titles beginning with "Pagan," 3 with "Primitive," and

4 with "Tribe" or "Tribal"), but not yet "fatally"-stricken in library subject-schema nor the mass media. (For a stunning recent demolition of "tribe," "primitive," "savage," "pagan," "barbarian," and like terms, see Okot p'Bitek's *African religions in Western scholarship,* lately issued by the East African Literature Bureau, especially pages 6–16, 20–23, and 44–46, as well as Professor Ali A. Mazrui's "Epilogue," in which—on page 124—he limns the refusal of Western scholars to acknowledge an African *civilization* and—on page 133—summarizes p'Bitek's objection to "primitive" as "being part of the general legitimation of imperial expansion itself...," for the proposition that "subject peoples were primitive ... was eminently convenient to rationalise the act of subjugating others.")

# FICTION ACCESS:
# NEW APPROACHES

Readers during the next decade, just as now, will want Regency novels; Poirot, Marple, and Maigret mysteries; occult spellbinders; and love stories. They'll crave George Smiley, James Bond, and Quiller intrigues. They'll continue to like Middle Earth, Narnian, and Ozian fantasies. They won't much care in 10 years — any more than at present — whether the yarns they seek happen to be published as single works or collections. And they may not remember particular authors or titles, associating Dracula, Holmes, or Hornblower with no specific writer or work.[1]

The question is: Will fiction fans have any more luck finding such stuff in the 80s than they did in the 70s? Or put another way: Must they remain just as frustrated in the new Silicon-Telematic Age as they were in Pre-Kilgourian Times? Of course, either today or tomorrow they might ask a knowledgeable librarian for a story with Marple, Maigret, or Oz in it. They might request a "Gothic," or something with a "regency" setting. But not *all* staffers are so fictionally "literate," and even standard reference tools like William Freeman's *Dictionary of fictional characters* (The Writer, 1974), Margery Fisher's *Who's who in children's books* (Holt, Rinehart and Winston, 1975), *The detectionary: a biographical dictionary of leading characters in detective and mystery fiction* (Overlook Press, 1977), Chris Steinbrunner and Otto Penzler's *Encyclopedia of mystery and detection* (McGraw-Hill, 1976), and Elsa J. Radcliffe's *Gothic novels of the Twentieth Century: an annotated bibliography* (Scarecrow Press, 1979) become quickly outdated and — in the aggregate — don't truly span the whole make-believe spectrum. Moreover, once authors and titles *have* been identified by memory or through searching aids, it must still be determined if the library's actually *got* the desired items. Another step. Another search. Another hang-up.

There must be an easier and better way to access fiction. A way to immediately identify what characters and other subjects are really represented in the collection. A way that simplifies life for reference and readers' advisory

*Reprinted with permission from* Reference Librarian, *nos. 1/2 (Fall/Winter 1981), pp. 45–53, where it originally appeared as "Reference, Readers, and Fiction: New Approaches."*

staff who may not be totally "tuned in" to Chewbacca, Thrush Green, and
Nancy Drew. A way to reduce patrons' dependence on intermediaries, to let
them become more bibliographically adventurous and self-reliant. And there
is such a way. It's through the catalog. Certainly not in most places. Not yet.
But in some. And it's definitely a method, a process, that's available for the
coming decade.

In conventional, LC-type cataloging, fiction typically gets few (if any)
subject tracings.[2] A *real,* historical person or event — like Theodore Roosevelt,
Bertrand Russell, or the French Revolution — sometimes garners a — FIC-
TION tracing if it figures prominently in the narrative, but imaginary
(although equally well-known) persons, groups, or places never enjoy such
treatments.[3] This double-standard represents a kind of bias that might be
called "fictionism." Further, genre-headings (e.g., DETECTIVE AND MYSTERY
STORIES, ISRAELI FICTION, and HORROR TALES) are usually applied *only* to
collections or anthologies, not to individual novels, films, or recordings.[4] And
the genre-thesaurus, in any event, is pathetically inadequate, completely failing to recognize such common categories as SPY FICTION, SUSPENSE STORIES,
and TALL TALES.

The need for improved access to novels, short stories, and their A/V
counterparts or versions has been stated publicly. More than once.[5] But the
Great Washington Behemoth either can't, or simply won't, respond. Given
that harsh fact, individual libraries anxious to better service *their own patrons
now* and not especially timid about altering or expanding Holy Outside Copy
*could* vault directly to The Eighties — without LC sanction or aid — by doing
several things themselves:

- Developing a thesaurus of descriptors for imaginary people, crea-
  tures, groups, and locales (providing they appear significantly in at
  least two published/filmed/recorded works), then assigning such rubrics with FICTION subheads: e.g., GULL, VLADIMIR — FICTION,
  WHITEOAK FAMILY — FICTION, ARTO DETOO — FICTION, SHANGRI-
  LA — FICTION. These headings should be established essentially like
  those for non-fiction, with normal and often "extra" cross-referencing;
  e.g.,

Bond, James.
  x Agent 007
    Double-0-Seven
    James Bond
    0-0-Seven
    Point-Zero-Zero-Seven
    Zero-Zero-Seven

Pibble, Jimmy.
  x Detective Superintendent Pibble

James Willoughby Pibble
Jimmy Pibble
Superintendent Pibble

Enterprise (Spaceship).
x Starship Enterprise

Fernald, Alvin.
x Alvin Fernald
"Magnificent Brain"

Marple, Miss Jane.
x Jane Marple
Miss Marple

Maigret, Jules.
x Inspector Maigret
Jules Maigret

Phin, Thackeray.
x Finn, Thackeray
Thackeray Phin

- Expanding the arsenal of genre-headings and making it a policy to assign suitable form-tracings to *all* fiction, both single works and collections.
- Applying purely topical and geographical descriptors (with — FICTION subheads) to *all* appropriate titles: e.g., AFRO-AMERICANS — FICTION, GARDENING — FICTION, ANDROIDS — FICTION, MIDDLE AGED MEN — FICTION, MULTINATIONAL CORPORATIONS — FICTION, THE THIRTIES — FICTION, TEENAGE PREGNANCY — FICTION, STRIKES — FICTION, GREED — FICTION, HOLLYWOOD, CALIFORNIA — FICTION, WOMEN EXECUTIVES — FICTION, DISABLED CHILDREN — FICTION, RACE RELATIONS — FICTION, MINNEAPOLIS — FICTION, GAY MEN — FICTION, RAPE — FICTION.

(This practice should ensure quick answers to nearly all "Do-you-have-a-story-about...?" queries.)

To help with thesaurus-building, here are the genre-headings currently employed at Hennepin County Library (HCL):

ADVENTURE STORIES
ANTI-WAR STORIES [ASSIGNED, E.G., TO DALTON TRUMBO'S *Johnny got his gun* (Lyle Stuart, 1979)]
ARGENTINE [ISRAELI, MEXICAN, etc.] FICTION
"BEAT" FICTION [assigned, e.g., to William S. Burroughs' *Naked lunch*

(Grove Press, 1966) and Jack Kerouac's *On the road* (Viking Press, 1957)]

CARTOON NOVELS [assigned, e.g., to Jules Feiffer's *Tantrum* (Knopf, 1979)]

CAUTIONARY TALES AND VERSE

CHINESE [FRENCH, SPANISH, TURKISH, etc.] FICTION [assigned, without subdivision, to foreign-language material]

ECO-FICTION [assigned, e.g., to Ernest Callenbach's *Ecotopia* (Banyan Tree Books, 1975) and Christopher Swan's *YV 88; an eco-fiction of tomorrow* (Sierra Club Books, 1977)]

EPIC FICTION

EPISTOLARY NOVELS [assigned, e.g., to John Barth's *Letters: a novel* (Putnam, 1979)]

EROTIC FICTION

FANTASY FICTION

FEMINIST FICTION [assigned, e.g, to Rita Mae Brown's *Rubyfruit jungle* (Daughters, 1973) and Charlotte Perkins Gilman's *Herland* (Feminist Press, 1973)]

GHOST STORIES

"GOTHIC" FICTION

GROTESQUE TALES

HISTORICAL ROMANCES

HORROR STORIES

HUMOROUS STORIES

LOVE STORIES

MELODRAMATIC FICTION

METAPHORICAL TALES

MYSTERY STORIES

OCCULT FICTION

PICARESQUE FICTION

PSYCHOLOGICAL FICTION

PULP FICTION

"REGENCY" NOVELS

ROMANTIC SUSPENSE STORIES

SATIRICAL FICTION

SCIENCE FICTION

SEA STORIES

SHORT STORIES

"SOAP OPERA" FICTION [assigned, e.g., to Cyra McFadden's *Serial: a year in the life of Marin County* (Knopf, 1977)]

SPY FICTION

STORIES WITHOUT WORDS

SURREALIST FICTION [assigned, e.g., to Kobo Abe's *Box man* (Knopf, 1974)]

SUSPENSE STORIES

SWASHBUCKLING TALES [assigned, e.g., to Kyril Bonfiglioli's *All the tea in China* (Pantheon Books, 1978), Alexandre Dumas' *Three musketeers* (Dutton, 1906), and Robert Kerr's *Dark lady* (Stein & Day, 1976)]

TALL TALES [assigned, e.g., to Albert S. Fleishman's *Jim Bridger's alarm clock, and other tall tales* (Dutton, 1978) and Ramona Maher's *When Windwagon Smith came to Westport* (Coward, McCann & Geoghegan, 1977)]

THEOLOGICAL FICTION

WAR STORIES

WESTERN STORIES

WORKING CLASS FICTION [assigned, e.g., to most Meridel LeSueur and Bruno Traven works, as well as Jack Conroy's *Writers in revolt* (Lawrence Hill, 1973) and Joseph North's *New Masses* (International Publishers, 1969)]

And this is a partial inventory of "unreal" HCL rubrics:

ADAMS, NICK
ALDEN FAMILY
AMELIA-BEDELIA
ANANSI
ANDERSON, EVERETT
ANHALT, MICI
APPLEBY, SIR JOHN
ARAGON, TOM
ARCHER, LEW
ARTHUR, KING
ARTOO DETOO
AUBREY, JACK
AUSTIN, STEVE
BABE THE BLUE OX
THE BARON
BECK, MARTIN
BEDE, SIMON
BEEF, WILLIAM
BELFORD, STACY
BENSON, BIG BULL
THE BERESFORDS
BLAISE, MODESTY
BLISS, VICKY
BOLITHO, RICHARD
BONAPARTE, INSPEC-
    TOR NAPOLEON

THE BORROWERS
BOUCHARD FAMILY
BRADLEY, DAME BEA-
    TRICE
BREDDER, FATHER JO-
    SEPH
BRENNAN, MICHAEL
BRODIE, PAUL
BROWN, FATHER
BROWN, LEROY
BRUNT, THOMAS
BUGS BUNNY
BULLOCK, HELEN
CARELLA, STEVE
CARRICK, WEBB
CARSON STREET DE-
    TECTIVE AGENCY
CARTER, NICK
THE CASPIANS
CASTANG, HENRI
CATFISH BEND
CHAMBRUN, PIERRE
CHEWBACCA
CHRISTIE, HESTER
CHRISTOPHER ROBIN
CLAUDINE

CONWAY, RUPERT
COYOTE THE TRICK-
    STER
DE GIER, RINUS
DEE JEN-DJIEH
DILLON, MATT
DON QUIXOTE
DORO
DORTMUNDER GANG
DOVER, WILFRED
DRACULA
DREW, NANCY
DUNN, DANNY
ENTERPRISE (SPACE-
    SHIP)
FANSLER, KATE
FELL, GIDEON
FEN, GERVASE
FERNALD, ALVIN
FIELDING, MADGE
FINN, HUCKLEBERRY
FLASHMAN, HARRY
    PAGET
FORTUNE, MARK
FRANKENSTEIN MON-
    STER

GHOTE, GANESH
GORDON, FLASH
GRANT, ALAN
GRAYMALKIN, MRS.
GREEN HORNET
GREY, ROMAN
GULL, VLADIMIR
GUTTMAN, MAX
HALFHYDE, ST. VIN-
  CENT
HARDY BOYS
HEFFERMAN, HOOKY
HEYDON, TOBEY
HOLMES, SHERLOCK,
  BORN 1854
HORNBLOWER, HORA-
  TIO
THE HULK
HUNTINGTON, COLIN
JEKYLL, HENRY
JERICHO, JOHN
JIVE, BILLY JO
JONES, GRAVE DIGGER
KAUFFMAN, MAX
KENT, PHILIP
KENWORTHY, SIMON
KRAMER, TROMPIE
KYD, THOMAS
LA NAGUE FEDERA-
  TION
LAND, HANNAH
LANIGAN, HUGH
LAY, LOUIE
LEAPHORN, JOE
LEIA, PRINCESS
LIAR, BILLY
LONE RANGER
LOVEJOY
LUGH THE HARPER
MC BROOM, JOSH
MC GARR, PETER
MC GEE, TRAVIS
MC GURK, JACK P.
MC KINLEY, MAGGIE

THE MADDOXES
MAIGRET, JULES
MAITLAND, ANTONY
MAKEPEACE, EMMA
MARLOWE, PHILLIP
MARPLE, MISS JANE
MASON, PERRY
MASUTO, MASAO
MAYO, ASEY
MEGAN
MENDOZA, LUIS
MEREWETHER, PERCI-
  VAL
MIDDLE-EARTH
MIGHTY MOUSE
MILLS, ADDIE
MONGO
MORAN, TOD
MORIARTY, JAMES,
  BORN 1846
MOSS, PHIL
MUFFIN, CHARLIE
MULLINER, MR.
NAPIER, CARSON
NARNIA
NASH, GEORGE
THE NORTHS
OAKES, BLACKFORD
OAKES, BOYSIE
OLMSTEAD, OX
OPARA, CHRISTIE
OZ
PADDINGTON-THE-
  BEAR
PALFREY, STANISLAUS
  ALEXANDER
PARIS, CHARLES
PECOS GANG
PELAZONI, LEXEY
  JANE
PELLUCIDAR
PENNINGTON, PA-
  TRICK
PETER PAN

PETERS, ANNA
PETERS, TOBY
PHILIS
PHIN, THACKERAY
PIBBLE, JIMMY
PICKERELL, MISS
PIGGLE-WIGGLE, MRS.
PINCH, DEARBORN V.
PINK, MELINDA
PIPPA MOUSE
POIROT, HERCULE
POLDARK FAMILY
POLLIFAX, EMILY
PONS, SOLAR
POPPINS, MARY
POWDER VALLEY,
  COLORADO
PRICE, HOMER
PRICE, POTTER AND
  PETACQUE, FIRM
QUARSHIE, DOCTOR
QUILLER (SECRET
  AGENT)
QUIMBY, RAMONA
QUIST, JULIAN
RAFFLES, A.J.
REACHFAR, SCOTLAND
REED, HENRY
REEDER, PAUL
REGAN, JACK
ROBERTSON, JEAN
ROGERS, BUCK
ROGERS, GEORGE
ROLFE, HELGA
ROOK, HOWIE
RUDD, INSPECTOR
RUDISILL, ROGER DE
SABER, SARAH
ST. IVES, PHILIP
SAMSON, ALBERT
SANCHEZ, ESPERANZA
SANTANGELO, MINNIE
SAVARD, BERNADETTE
SCROOGE, EBENEZER

| | | |
|---|---|---|
| SEVERANCE, GRACE | STAUNTON, BOB | VAN DER VALK, IN- |
| THE SHADOW | STERN, HANNIBAL | SPECTOR |
| SHAFT, JOHN | STRANGEWAYS, NIGEL | VAN DUSEN, AUGUS- |
| SHANE, COLIN | STREGA NONA | TUS S.F.X. |
| SHANGRI-LA | SUNSET, SUSIE | VELVET, NICK |
| SHAPIRO, NATHAN | TARZAN | WILDE, JONAS |
| SHAUGHNESSY, MARY | TEATIME, LUCILLA | WATSON, JOHN HAM- |
| ANN | EDITH CAVELL | ISH, BORN 1852 |
| SHAYNE, MICHAEL | THATCHER, JOHN | WEST, ROGER |
| SHOMAR, SHOMRI | PUTNAM | WHITEOAK FAMILY |
| SILK, DORIAN | THORNDYKE, JOHN | WILLUM, PERSIS |
| SKYWALKER, LUKE | EVELYN | WIMSEY, LORD PETER |
| SMALL, DAVID | THREE INVESTIGATORS | WINNIE-THE-POOH |
| SMILEY, GEORGE | THRUSH GREEN, EN- | WITHERS, HILDE- |
| SMOKEY THE BEAR | GLAND | GARDE |
| SOLDEN, ANNA | TIBBETT, HENRY | WOLFE, NERO |
| SOLO, HAN | TIBBS, VIRGIL | WOODLAWN, CADDIE |
| SORENSEN FAMILY | THE TOFF | WOODY WOODPECKER |
| SPADE, SAM | TONKO | WOOSTER, BERTRAM |
| SPENCE, BEN | TUCKER, KATIE JOHN | WYNDSOR, BERTRAM |
| SPOCK, MR. | VADER, DARTH | ZARKON, LORD OF |
| STABLE, GEORGE | VAN DER VALK, AR- | THE UNKNOWN |
| STANTON, WILL | LETTE | ZONDI, MICKEY |
| STARBUCK, OBAKIAH | | |

These "new approaches" work. And they can easily be implemented in all genuinely "popular" libraries.

As the 21st Century nears and pressure mounts for libraries and other institutions to operate on a more decentralized, people-responsive, "human" scale, the sure satisfaction of future users should clearly transcend or nullify the terrible "sin" of deviating from past orthodoxy and inertia. Enlarging access to the recreational and sometimes instructive, if not also inspiring, world of imagination seems a worthy "deviation."

## NOTES

1. Says critic Robert Sorensen: "Some fictional sleuths tend to be born as Hitlerian puppets, tiny wooden Frankenstein monsters who quickly see the bright lights and decide to sever all ties with their dull ventriloquist masters. As the ingrates carve out their own empires on library shelves, *their creators may be all but forgotten.* One amazing result of this is that we probably have more biographies of the characters than of their creators!" See "In my book...," *Minneapolis tribune,* Feb. 19, 1978, p. 15D. Emphasis added. What Sorensen neglected to mention is that those "creators" might also have multiplied in the meantime as imitators or successors in effect produce "born again" characters no longer associated solely with one original author. The archetypal example: Sherlock Holmes, who stays

vibrantly "alive," pursuing Moriarty and other underworld sorts in ever-*new* books, films, and plays, although Conan Doyle, his progenitor, *died 50 years ago.*

2. According to Bohdan S. Wynar, "The Library of Congress presently adds an average of 2.3 subject entries per cataloged item. *This figure includes those titles for which no subject headings are assigned (e.g., individual works of* drama, *fiction,* poetry, and the like)." See "Verbal subject analysis," in his *Introduction to cataloging and classification* (6th ed.; Libraries Unlimited, 1980), p. 489. Emphasis added.

3. For examples, see *Library of Congress catalog; books: subjects,* 1965-1969 (J.W. Edwards, 1979), v. 15, p. 567; "Baker Street blackout," *HCL cataloging bulletin,* no. 40 (May/June 1979), pp. 1-2; and S. Berman's "Proposed: a subject cataloging code for public and school libraries," *HCL cataloging bulletin,* no. 39 (March/April 1979), p. 4; "Catalogue of horrors," *Emergency librarian,* v. 4, no. 4 (March/April 1977), pp. 8, 10; and "Access to alternatives," *Collection building,* v. 2, no. 2 (March 1980), pp. 38-9, 43, 46, 51. Also: Berman's remarks following William J. Welsh's presentation at the 1975 ISAD Cataloging Institute, in *Nature and future of the catalog* (Oryx Press, 1979), p. 79.

4. For the latest LC policy statement, see "Fiction in subject heading practice," *Cataloging Service bulletin,* no. 122 (Summer 1977), pp. 11-13. With respect to "individual works of fiction," the governing rule is to "assign no form [i.e., genre] heading to any work," while topical rubrics may be applied merely to "biographical" and "historical" titles, together with "animal stories." For a codification of LC literary-praxis, see Lois Mai Chan, "Subject areas requiring special treatment: literature," in her *Library of Congress subject headings* (Libraries Unlimited, 1978), pp. 213-25.

5. See, for instance, Marvin H. Scilken's "Catalog as a public service tool," in *Nature and future of the catalog,* p. 92, and "Demystifying the catalogue," *Emergency librarian,* v. 4, no. 4 (March/April 1977), p. 5. Also: S. Berman's "Cataloging for public libraries," in *Nature and future of the catalog,* pp. 228-29; "Ethnic access," *HCL cataloging bulletin,* no. 35 (July/Aug. 1978), p. 6; and "Gay access," *Gay insurgent,* nos. 4/5 (Spring 1979), pp. 14-15. More recently, Stephen MacDonald complained: "Another serious problem with libraries as a source of positive and affirming material [on homosexuality] is that a catalogue search will invariably turn up only non-fiction titles on the topic." See "Young, Gay and the problem of self identity: an annotated bibliography," *Emergency librarian,* v. 8, no. 1 (Sept./Oct. 1980), p. 8.

## FURTHER SOURCES

"Film and literary genres: a checklist of HCL headings," *HCL cataloging bulletin,* no. 26 (Feb. 1, 1977), p. 25.

*HCL cataloging bulletin.* 1973 — Bimonthly. $12/institutions, $6/individuals; back issues @ $1.50.
    Reports fictional and other subject heading innovations.

*Hennepin County Library authority file.* 1977 — Quarterly. $30 p.a., $7.50 single cumulations.
    42x microfiche service, containing all HCL name and subject headings, with notes and cross-references. Orders to: Secretary, Technical Services Division, Hennepin County Library, 12601 Ridgedale Drive, Minnetonka MN 55343.

*Hennepin County Library catalog.* 6th ed. 1980. 13 volumes.
    For "GOTHIC" FICTION entries, e.g., see v. 5, pp. 3229-32; "REGENCY" NOVELS, v. 10, pp. 6370-71; and HOLMES, SHERLOCK, BORN 1854 — FICTION, v. 6, p. 3655.

"Out of the closet," *Acquisitive librarian,* v. 2, no. 9 (May 1, 1980), p. 5.
    News note on subject cataloging Regency novels at HCL and OPL (Orange, New Jersey, Public Library).

"Some of our best friends are unreal: an assortment of HCL headings for fictional people, places, and things," *HCL cataloging bulletin,* no. 33 (March/April 1978), pp. 1-3.

Thompson, Steve, "Feedback," *HCL cataloging bulletin,* no. 25 (Dec. 1, 1976), pp. 1–2. The editor's reply to this letter not only addresses the touchy matter of name-forms for Holmesian characters, but also explains — with examples — how to handle material that "discusses, interprets, or analyzes" fictional persons.

# FICTION ACCESS (CONTINUED)

Libraries unhappy with the present niggardly cataloging of novels and short stories may find Hennepin County Library rubrics useful in expanding — indeed, exploding — access to fictional genres, places, and characters. These are headings innovated since the basic list published in "Reference, Readers and Fiction: New Approaches."

## Genres

MOVIE NOVELS
[assigned, e.g., to Richard J. Anobile's *Official Rocky Horror Picture Show Movie Novel* (1980)]

"RAGS-TO-RICHES" STORIES
[assigned, e.g., to Desiree Meyler's *Forget Tomorrow* (1981) and various Horatio Alger titles]

SAMIZDAT FICTION
[assigned, e.g., to Venedikt Erofeev's *Moscow to the End of the Line* (1980)]

## Characters and Places

| | | |
|---|---|---|
| ALVAREZ, ENRIQUE | BOBBSEY TWINS | CHAMISA CITY, NEW |
| AMES, RICH | BOORI | MEXICO |
| ANDERSON, EINSTEIN | BRANESTAWN, PRO- | CHESTER CRICKET |
| ANGELIQUE | FESSOR | CHILLY WILLY |
| ANGSTROM, HARRY | BUMPPO, NATTY | CHINGACHGOOK |
| BABAR | CADFAEL, BROTHER | CHISHOLM, CATRIONA |
| BECKMAN, HOLLY | CAINE, NICK | CROMWELL, BILL |
| BINTON, MARGARET | CALRISSIAN, LANDO | DAMIOT, INSPECTOR |

*Reprinted from* Technicalities, *v. 2, no. 7 (July 1982), pp. 7, 16, by permission of M.E. Sharpe, Inc., Armonk NY 10504.*

DARKOVER [planet]
DAVIDSON, SAM
DECKER, RAY
DEENE, CAROLUS
DEVENTER, PIET
DOOLITTLE, DOCTOR
EDEN FAMILY
EPTON, ROSA
FALKENSTEIN, JESSE
FINNEY, BARBARA
FRANCINE [creator:
 Marc Brown]
GAUTIER, JEAN-PAUL
GAYLEIGH, PETER
GLASS FAMILY
GLOOSCAP
GODFREY, CHRIS
GORDON, ALISON B.
GORDON, YUDEL
GRAND FENWICK
 [duchy]
GREENFIELD, C.B.
GUINNESS, RAY
HALL, PHILIP
HATCHER, FARLEY
 DREXEL [x "Fudge"
 Hatcher]
HATCHER, PETER
HATCHER, TOOTSIE
HENRY (SIAMESE CAT)
HEYDON, MIDGE
HIGHTOWER, BESSIE
HONEYBATH,
 CHARLES
ISLANDIA
JAHDU
JAMESON, DANNY
JAMESON, JACK
KHE'CHIN

KILDARE, JAMES [x
 Dr. Kildare]
KNIGHT, SAM
KOESLER, FATHER
 ROBERT
KRALES, JOSH
KRUPNIK, ANASTASIA
LAMBERT, BETH
LAVETTE FAMILY
LEITH, LESTER
LEWIS, MARCY
LISTER, JOHNNY
LITTLEJOHN, CHIEF
 SUPERINTENDENT
LOGAN, TOM
LORIMER FAMILY
MCKAY FAMILY
MCLAUGHLIN FAMILY
MACLEAN, GREGOR
MARKS, BOBBY
MARY TERESA, SISTER
MISS PIGGY
MORETTI, PADDY
MORTDECAI, CHARLIE
MOWGLI
NUMENOR
PARKER [creator:
 Richard Stark]
PAY, EBEN
PERONE, ACHILLE
PETTRELLA, PATRICK
PINAUD, M.
PINCUS, "SILKY"
PINKERTON FAMILY
PITT, DIRK
QUACKENBUSH, WIL-
 BUR
REINHART, CARL

RHYS, MADOC
ROBAK, DON
ROBINSON, DAN
ROBINSON FAMILY
ROSHER, DETECTIVE
RYAN, JOSEPH "VON"
SAVAGE FAMILY
SCHWEIK, JOSEF [x
 Good Soldier
 Schweik]
SCUDDER, MATTHEW
SEVERIAN
SHARPE, RICHARD
SHIRLEY, ANNE
SILVER, ARIZONA JIM
SIMON, MARGARET
SINBAD [dog]
SOSSI, ALDO
STEVENSON, FAMILY
TALLON, JACK
TANNER, JOHN
TICHY, IJON
TONTO
TOYE, GREGORY
TREEHORN [creator:
 Florence Parry]
TROTTER, TILLY
TWITE, DIDO
WALKER, AMOS
WINNETOU
WYND FAMILY
YODA
YOK-YOK
YOKNAPATAWPHA
 COUNTY, MISSIS-
 SIPPI
YOWDER, XENON
 ZEBULON

And a sample authority file entry:

Yowder, Xenon Zebulon.

cn Fictional character. Creator: Glen Rounds.

x Mr. Yowder
  Xenon Zebulon Yowder
  Yowder, Mr.

# A BONNIE SCREW-UP

These are the basics:

Author: Daisy Vivian

Title: *Rose White, Rose Red*

Publisher: Walker and Company

Date: 1983

Jacket subtitle: "A romance of Georgian England."

Jacket blurb: "...Young Blanche Montague ... certainly doesn't expect to become involved in the clandestine doings of the group of high-born Jacobites actively plotting to put Bonnie Prince Charlie on the English throne."

CIP subject tracing: 1. Great Britain—History—Jacobite Rebellions, 1765—Fiction. MARC subject tracing: 1. Great Britain—History—Wars of the Roses, 1455-1485—Fiction.

While it's nice that the opus got subject cataloged at all—a rarity for fiction—the treatment defies belief:

- The CIP subject heading doesn't appear in LCSH. Nowhere. In short, it's not legit.

- No Jacobite rebellions went down in 1765. The last military effort to restore the Stuarts was at Culloden in 1746. Charlie's boys lost. Thus, the CIP rubric would be inaccurate even if it *did* appear in LCSH. And, in any event, no "rebellion" occurs in Vivian's story. Only plotting. (Which, by the way, makes LCSH's 3 JACOBITE REBELLION forms inapplicable.)

- The second-try heading ideally should have corrected the erroneous CIP tracing, but instead placed the action in a period nearly 2 centuries *earlier* than the actual time-setting (i.e., shortly after the Second Jacobite Rebellion of 1745-46).

To recap: Although single novels don't ordinarily receive much, if any, attention from LC subject catalogers, this one seems to have been worked on twice, with 2 entirely different results. However, neither assigned tracing fits the work, and one (perhaps composed by the publisher?) not only can't be

*Reprinted from* Technicalities, *v. 4, no. 8 (August 1984), pp. 8, 11, by permission of M.E. Sharpe, Inc., Armonk NY 10504.*

found in the LC thesaurus, but also denotes "historical" events that never happened.

With the admitted benefit of hindsight, this is how Hennepin County subject-traced the book:

1. Great Britain—History—George II, 1727–1760—Fiction.
2. Jacobites—Fiction.
3. Historical romances.
4. Eighteenth Century—Fiction.

Incidentally, to compound the farce, the rear jacket features this quote from Marian Seldes:

"Until I read Daisy Vivian's *Rose White, Rose Red,* I was a virgin. It was my first Regency romance...."

Regency romances, of course, take place *only* during the 1811–1820 decade, more than 50 years *later* than Blanche Montague caroused with those "high-born Jacobites." So Marian may still be a virgin.

# WHERE HAVE ALL
# THE MOONIES GONE?

According to the Good Book, Chapter 24, Verse 1: "Enter a corporate body directly under the name by which it is predominantly identified.... Determine the form of name of a corporate body from items issued by that body in its language...."[1] Doubtless, Library of Congress (LC) cataloguers faithfully and properly applied that rule when constructing corporate name-forms—which, incidentally, also serve as subject headings—for Lech Walesa's now-banned labor federation and Reverend Moon's religious organization. That is, they must have examined materials produced in the home language—Polish and Korean—and determined the "predominant" form of name in each language. So, instead of "Solidarity," we find in MARC and CIP entries, "NSZZ 'Solidarnosc.'" And, rather than "Unification Church," we get "Segye Kidokkyo T'ongil Sillyong Hyophoe." Let's call these Exhibit A.

In June 1982, Temple University Press issued a 521-page, triple-column anthology, *Alternative Papers*,[2] containing about 200 reprinted articles arranged into 11 sections:
- The Press
- Nukes
- Appropriate Technology
- Third World
- Corporate Connections
- Repression
- Women
- Lesbians & Gay Men
- Work
- Organizing
- The Movement

What would seem a decent minimum of subject tracings? Perhaps RADICALISM, SOCIAL MOVEMENTS, and SOCIAL CHANGE? Maybe also THIRD

*Reprinted with permission from* Reference Librarian, *no. 9 (Fall/Winter 1983), pp. 133–43.*

WORLD, NUCLEAR POWER, FEMINISM, GAY LIBERATION MOVEMENT, and
ALTERNATIVE PRESS PUBLICATIONS — EXCERPTS?[3] What subject tracings did
it actually get? None. Nada. Zip. Nichts. Call that Exhibit B.

At a Twin Cities' conference in late 1982, people like Harlan Cleveland,
Toni Carbo Bearman, Paul Zurkowski, and Anita Schiller talked about "information as a resource and commodity," particularly discussing the merits
and possible implications of the NCLIS Task Force report on private sec-
tor/public sector responsibilities.[4] During that weekend event, certain
notable themes or topics recurred:

- FEE-BASED INFORMATION SERVICES
- GOVERNMENT PUBLISHING POLICY
- INFORMATION INDUSTRY
- INFORMATION POLICY
- INFORMATION SOCIETY
- TELEMATICS

Most libraries have material on those subjects. The Awful Truth, though, is
that in most libraries such material cannot be identified nor retrieved through
the catalog by means of those terms. Because they haven't been validated yet
as nationally-acceptable headings by LC. That's Exhibit C.

In 1982, Little, Brown published what the jacket blurb described as an
"adventure-filled memoir" by Robert MacNeil, co-host of PBS' *MacNeil-Lehrer
Report.* Titled *The Right Place at the Right Time,* the work was classed in
813.54 — i.e., contemporary American fiction — and accordingly got no subject headings.[5] Make that Exhibit D.

As Exhibit E: Marilyn Sachs' juvie novel, *Call Me Ruth,* appeared in 1982
(published by Doubleday). The jacket says: "A warm and moving story about
the struggles of a young Jewish immigrant in New York City at the turn of
the century." And the first page of text includes these passages:

In the old country, my name was Rifka and my mother's name was Faigel.
But when we came to America, I became Ruth and my mother became
Fanny. . . . Mamma was standing bare-legged in the water, her skirts hiked
up around her waist, rinsing off the large, white Passover tablecloth, for the
holiday had just ended.

Okay. THIS is the annotation supplied by LC's juvenalia catalogers:

The daughter of a Russian immigrant family, newly arrived in Manhattan
in 1908, has conflicting feelings about her mother's increasingly radical
union involvement.

And this is the first — and only ethnic-related — subject tracing: RUSSIAN
AMERICANS — FICTION.[6]

Well, the "exhibits" could continue to "Z" and beyond. The object in this
litany of error and omission should be fairly transparent: to weaken confidence in centrally-performed cataloging and standard cataloging tools. Not
for any personal nor mean-minded reasons, but simply because the fact is that
our national cataloging products and services can't be completely trusted and

should not be accepted automatically nor uncritically by anyone who genuinely believes that cataloging should make material *more* rather than *less* accessible and retrievable.

To become more systematic: these are three basic principles that ought to underpin cataloging:

- *Intelligibility:* The catalog format, entry-elements, and terminology should make sense, should be understandable not just by staff, but also by ordinary patrons.
- *Findability:* Ideally, searchers should be able to "hit" what they want, especially when subject searching or author-browsing, on the first try.
- *Fairness:* Various *kinds* of materials — like print-AV and adult-juvenile — should be treated equitably; subject nomenclature should be unbiased; subject coverage should be fullsome, especially for women's, ethnic, sexual, political, and age-connected materials; and individual works deserve accurate representation, together with maximum accessibility.

Now, with those principles as a basis for evaluation, here's what's "wrong" — that is, dysfunctional and unhelpful — in currently-practiced descriptive and subject cataloging:

## DESCRIPTIVE CATALOGING

### Choice-of-entry

The new rules mandate entry of story or essay collections under title, rather than under editor or compiler.[7] So *Before the Golden Age: a Science Fiction Anthology of the 1930s,* compiled by Isaac Asimov, would be main-entried under "Before." Does that really make any difference? It does. Both studies and personal observation strongly suggest that people look for a *name* associated with a given work, not the title, and that they don't make fine distinctions between monographs and edited collections.[8] The practical effect of this AACR2 rule is to dictate shelf-location among the "Bs" instead of "As," where fiction-browsers might reasonably be looking for "Asimov" items. And in single-entry catalogs, the title would be the *sole* entry point.

### Punctuation/Abbreviations

While not wishing to re-hash earlier debates, it still needs to be said that typical library users do not comprehend what "[s.l.]" or "[s.n.]" means, and that a significant number of users and staff alike plainly don't understand such cherished, long-standing bibliographic conventions as "min.," "b&w," "pt.," "in.," "b." (for "born"), "l." (for "leaves"), "d." (for "died"), "v.," "tr.," and "c" (for "copyright"). A 1979 Hennepin County Library survey strongly supported this.[9] And an earlier study regarding AV-abbreviations, conducted among Wisconsin college and high school students, did likewise.[10] If these sorts of data are important enough to include in a catalog entry, then they're important enough to be made comprehensible.

## Notes

Non-archival libraries don't need some standard notes like "Includes index" or "Includes bibliography." However, other sorts of notes could prove extremely useful in helping potential readers decide whether they truly want a particular item, but these are less frequently supplied. For instance, HCL catalogers added this note to the record for Gloria Kaufman's *Pulling Our Own Strings: Feminist Humor and Satire:* "Includes anecdotes, songs, cartoons, poetry, essays, jokes, and comic routines." And they regularly make notes about sequels and cycles; e.g., "The 2d volume of the author's Dirshan The God-Killer saga, the 1st of which is The Lerious mecca, the 3d, Sword for the empire, and the 4th, The maneaters of Cascalon." Further, "Includes more than 50 photos, some in color, and over 70 traditional designs and projects to piece by machine and quilt in your lap," seems more likely to aid erstwhile borowers than LC's cryptic collation for the same work:[11] "ill. (some col.)."

## Added Entries

While not explicitly prohibited by the rules, a variety of helpful added entries simply don't get made — unless they're done locally. At HCL, for example, public service staff and patrons appreciate added entries for small, alternative, and regional presses, for notable people who contribute forewords or prefaces, for translators and illustrators, and for professional or community groups associated with a given work. Also, HCL catalogers routinely make title added entries for pieces of titles or rearranged titles *if* there's cause to believe that people might seek that entry-point. To illustrate: the orthodox title tracing for Wayne Dyer's 1976 best-seller, *Your Erroneous Zones*, was purely for "Your," filing in the Ys. But HCL made another for what may be the much more memorable permuted title: "Erroneous zones," filing in the Es.[12]

## Form-of-heading #1

The "Solidarity" and "Unification Church" cases nicely exemplify this kind of dysfunctional rule. Nobody will score a "first hit" because nobody will look first under "NSZZ" or "Segye." And many libraries, for whatever reason, will not have introduced cross-references from the sensible forms to the *insen*-sible ones, so the material may be permanently hidden and irretrievable. Obviously, either the rule should be revised to mandate name-establishment according to the predominant form in the language of the country where the material is being cataloged[13] or, paraphrasing George Orwell, a caution should appear in boldface at the bottom of every AACR2 page: **BREAK ANY OF THESE RULES SOONER THAN CREATE AN OUTRIGHT BARBAROUS ENTRY.**

*Form-of-heading #2*

AACR2 Rule 22.2C (p. 351) belatedly, but justly, liberated Sholem Aleichem, Orwell, Moravia, Celine, and Stendhal from a kind of bibliographic imprisonment, a confinement under the "real" names that they hadn't actually used when writing and that most readers wouldn't easily recognize, much less search for, in a catalog or on the shelves. This is Rule 22.2C1:

> If all the works by a person appear under one pseudonym, or if the person is predominantly identified in reference sources by one pseudonym, choose the pseudonym. If the real name is known, make a reference from the real name to the pseudonym.

That departure from the "real name" tradition represented a genuine improvement in catalog access and credibility. Indeed, it was a significant step toward demystification. (Why, for so many years, did the profession insist that patrons look under "Rabinowitz" or "Blair" or "Pincherle" or "Destouches" or "Beyle" when only "Aleichem," "Orwell," "Moravia," "Celine" and "Stendhal" appeared on title pages, on covers, on spines, on dust jackets, in reviews, and in bibliographies?) If Rule 22.2C1 ("One pseudonym") may be rightly regarded as a great advance, Rule 22.2C2— nestled just below it (pp. 351-2)—cannot. Captioned "Predominant name," it reads:

> If the works of a person appear under several pseudonyms (or under the real name and one or more pseudonyms), choose one of those names if the person has come to be identified predominantly by that name in later editions of his or her works, or in other reference sources (in that order of preference). Make references from the other names.

The practical outcome of this instruction is that while novels in the Lavette Family saga by Howard Fast are expectably and properly entered under "Fast, Howard" and therefore shelved among the Fs, the Masao Masuto mysteries by E.V. Cunningham (a Fast pseudonym) are *also* entered under "Fast, Howard" and similarly shelved among the Fs. How come? Presumably because the author has written *more* works as "Fast" than as "Cunningham." The name form (and consequent shelf-location) thus derives from mathematics, not from common sense or utility. And the result is just as foolish and dysfunctional as the earlier "real name" practice. It could, of course, have been obviated if the rule-makers had merely validated the principle of "title-page cataloging."[14]

## SUBJECT CATALOGING

One aspect of the subject cataloging problem is assignment practice, demonstrated by the *Alternative Papers* and *Call Me Ruth* examples. To *Alternative Papers* LC catalogers applied no vocabulary, and to *Call Me Ruth* they applied the wrong vocabulary. Still another defect inheres in LC assignment-policy regarding fiction, poetry, essays, humor, drama, and letters. Rarely, apart from adult anthologies and children's books, do such literary works get either topical or genre headings. (Robin MacNeil's richly-thematic memoir almost certainly went headingless due to its mistaken classification as "Fiction," an error that probably stemmed from cataloging "front matter" instead of the book itself during the CIP process.)[15] But school and public libraries, in particular, could greatly benefit from precisely such subject access to individual novels, plays, and other literature.[16]

While there's much to complain about concerning assignment, the vocabulary itself probably constitutes the largest part of the subject cataloging malaise. To begin with, too many active, primary headings remain awkward, archaic, or unfamiliar. They are terms not likely to be "first" sought by catalog users. For example:

| *LC form* | *Common form* |
|---|---|
| AERONAUTICS — ACCIDENTS | AIRPLANE ACCIDENTS |
| CARGO SHIPS — PASSENGER TRAVEL | FREIGHTER TRAVEL |
| CLOTHING, COLD WEATHER | WINTER CLOTHING |
| DWELLINGS | HOUSES |
| INFORMAL SECTOR (ECONOMICS) | UNDERGROUND ECONOMY |
| MICROMYS MINUTUS | HARVEST MOUSE |
| MILITARY SERVICE, COMPULSORY | DRAFT |
| MOVING PICTURE INDUSTRY — COLLECTIBLES | FILM COLLECTIBLES |
| ORTHODOX EASTERN CHURCH, GREEK | GREEK ORTHODOX CHURCH |
| PARENTING — RELIGIOUS ASPECTS — CHRISTIANITY | CHRISTIAN PARENTING |
| TRADE UNIONS | LABOR UNIONS |

Secondly, a number of palpably biased or inauthentic descriptors persist in standard thesauri. MAN has not yet been transmuted into HUMANS. Alien ethnonyms still denote the Inuit and Sami. And neither JEWISH QUESTION nor YELLOW PERIL have been reformed or replaced.[17]

Thirdly, and most critical, is a continuing failure to promptly recognize and legitimize new topics, as well as finally validating "old" ones. Among the "old":

BROWN LUNG DISEASE
CLASSICAL MUSIC[18]

FAMILY PLANNING
HOME REMEDIES
HUMAN SERVICES
INTEREST RATES
MARXISM
NEW LEFT
PARTICIPATORY MANAGEMENT
POLLUTION CONTROL

And among the "new":

ANTI-PORNOGRAPHY MOVEMENT
"BABY BOOM" GENERATION
CHRISTIAN BROADCASTING
DIVORCE MEDIATION SERVICES
HOMOPHOBIA
NEW AGE
NEW FEDERALISM
NEW RIGHT
NUCLEAR FREEZE CAMPAIGN
SAGEBRUSH REBELLION
SMALL BUSINESS LOANS
STARCH-BLOCKER DIET
TUITION TAX CREDIT
VIDEO DISPLAY TERMINALS
VIOLENCE AGAINST WOMEN
WELLNESS LIFESTYLE

If it's agreed that at least some of these things are really "wrong" with cataloging—and we take cataloging seriously—what's to be done? Well, there's no instant "fix." For instance, replacing LC subject headings with another system, like PRECIS, won't miraculously make subject cataloging "work." In fact, the same people would be applying and developing the new system who made a mess out of the old one. And the impact on existing subject catalogs could easily be disastrous. Nor is there a technological "fix." Merely changing from a card to an online catalog doesn't automatically change the *content* of the cataloging nor will it fully compensate for the lack of a good, modern, controlled vocabulary and user-oriented descriptive data. So what then? It may be hard medicine, but we *can* do two things, "inside" and "outside."

*Outside:* If we can identify a product or policy that's not working but can be repaired, we should let the responsible parties know about it. With respect to that "Solidarity" rule, it would be a matter of communicating—either individually or through professional groups—with the appropriate LC office and ALA committee. It's most effective to precisely specify what's wrong—and propose a remedy. (That goes for subject headings, too.) And it would be wise to publicize your communications in the library press. The more publicity, the more leverage, and the greater chance of getting things changed.

*Inside:* While admittedly tougher, given staff and money cuts everywhere, it's a matter of critically examining—and, when necessary, altering—"outside copy," as in the Robin MacNeil case. It's a matter of locally creating and assigning subject headings when you need them.[19] And it's a matter of trying to perform as much catalog maintenance as possible, especially adding essential cross-references between subject and name forms.[20]

To sum up: The Moonies haven't gone anywhere. It only seems that way. Which is lamentable. But also correctible.

## NOTES

1. The "Good Book": *Anglo-American Cataloguing Rules.* 2d ed. (Chicago: American Library Association, 1978). For "Basic Rule" 24.1, see p. 402.

2. Edited by Elliott Shore, Patricia J. Case, and Laura Daly.

3. Except that LC employs UNDERDEVELOPED AREAS and ATOMIC ENERGY instead of THIRD WORLD and NUCLEAR POWER. ALTERNATIVE PRESS PUBLICATIONS, of course, would be an altogether new heading.

4. *Public Sector/Private Sector Interaction in Providing Information Services: Report to the NCLIS* (Washington, DC: GPO, 1982).

5. The error has since been corrected. The current MARC record shows the title is classed in PN 4874 and 070.924 (biographies of journalists).

6. For more on how LC mis-cataloged this work, see my "'Jewish Question' in Subject Cataloging (Continued)," *Technicalities,* v. 3, no. 1 (Jan. 1983), p. 9, and v.3, no. 3 (March 1983), p. 6.

7. See AACR2 Rule 21.1C, p. 286.

8. See, for instance, Phyllis A. Richmond, "The AACR, Second Edition, What Next?," in Maurice J. Freedman and S. Michael Malinconico, editors, *The Nature and Future of the Catalog* (Phoenix: Oryx Press, 1979), pp. 192-3.

9. See Larry Legus, "Sure, They Save Space, But Who Knows What They Mean?" *HCL Cataloging Bulletin,* no. 40 (May/June 1979), pp. 24-9.

10. Jane Schlueter and Robert D. Little, "The Mystery of Ips and Mono; Or, Do Students Understand AV Card Catalog Terms?" *Wisconsin Library Bulletin,* Nov./Dec. 1973, pp. 381-3.

11. The work: *Lap quilting with Georgia Bonesteel* (Oxmoor House, 1982).

12. For more on title added entries, see my "Title Access: the Need, the Policy, and the Practice," *Technicalities,* v. 1, no. 1 (Dec. 1980), pp. 6-7; Janet Swann Hill, "Letters to the editor," *ibid.,* v. 1, no. 2 (Jan. 1981), p. 2; my response to Hill, *ibid.,* v. 1, no. 4 (1981), p. 2; and my "Missing Titles," *ibid.,* v. 2, no. 3 (March 1982), p. 11.

13. On March 24, 1983, at the PLA National Conference in Baltimore, I made this "action-recommendation" to the Cataloging Needs of Public Libraries Committee: Replace the 2d paragraph of Rule 24.1 ("Determine the form of name of a corporate body from items issued by that body in its language...") with: "Determine the form of name of a corporate body from items issued by or about that body in the language of the country where those items are being cataloged, provided that the translation is a true rendering of the original name."

14. The principle can still be fully validated by means of this proposal, also made in Baltimore: "Compress Rules 22.2C1 (One Pseudonym), 22.2C2 (Predominant name), and

22.2C3 (No predominant name) into a single instruction: If the works of a person appear under one pseudonym, under several pseudonyms, or under the real name and one or more pseudonyms, enter each work under the name specifically associated with it, making references from and to the person's other names.

15. This continuing situation prompted another Baltimore suggestion: Institute stringent quality control at the Library of Congress, ensuring that LC catalogers and classifiers work from substantial, if not full, galleys rather than frequently misleading and inaccurate "front matter." See also my "Time to Blow the Whistle on CIP," *Technicalities,* v. 3, no. 4 (April 1983), p. 6.

16. For more on theory and methods, see my "Reference, Readers and Fiction: New Approaches," *Reference Librarian,* nos. 1/2 (Fall/Winter 1981), pp. 45–53, later updated in "Fiction Access," *Technicalities,* v. 2, no. 7 (July 1982), pp. 7, 16.

17. For further discussion, examples, and sourcelists, see my *Prejudices and Antipathies* (Metuchen, NJ: Scarecrow Press, 1971); "Access/Equity," in *Joy of Cataloging* (Phoenix: Oryx Press, 1981), pp. 61–155; and "Where Have All the Women Gone?," *Technicalities,* v. 2, no. 12 (Dec. 1982), p. 15; v. 3, no. 1 (Jan. 1983), p. 10; v. 3, no. 2 (Feb. 1982), p. 11.

18. Randall W. Scott addressed the "classical music" issue in "Sour Notes," *Technicalities,* v. 2, no. 4 (April 1982), p. 9.

19. For aids and ideas, see "Do-It-Yourself Subject Cataloging: Sources and Tools," *Library Journal,* April 15, 1982, pp. 785–6, later updated in *Technicalities,* v. 2, no. 6 (June 1982), p. 8; v. 2, no. 8 (Sept. 1982), p. 7.

20. In some catalogs, for instance, material is subject traced under either NEAR EAST or MIDDLE EAST — i.e., *both* terms appear in the catalog — but there's no link, no connection, made between the two sequences.

# TITLE ACCESS:
# THE NEED, THE POLICY,
# AND THE PRACTICE

*The Need*

In 1971, Marvin Scilken, director of the Orange (New Jersey) Public Library, declared that "most users of library catalogs are looking for specific books. It is my observation," he continued, "that many clients may catch words out of a title and look for the book by these catchwords."[1] Accordingly, Scilken's own library "has filed cards under catchwords, subtitles, synthetic subtitles, permuted titles, or anything that might help a reader find a book. Even common misspellings are filed."[2]

Catalog use studies abundantly confirm Scilken's views about searching behavior and the value of added entries for permuted or catch-titles. For instance, these title-related items appear among the major research findings lately synthesized by Pauline Atherton:

• People often remember key words in titles even when they do not remember exact titles.[3]

• Permuted title indexes greatly raise the success rate of searching for incomplete and half-remembered titles.[4]

• Future catalogs should incorporate principles of redundancy and multiple-access routes to a much greater extent than they do presently. Unquestionably, title entries are of special importance, with each word accessible as a separate alphabetic entry with suitable provision for entry by means of singular/plural and other types of word-form variations, as well as synonyms.[5]

*Reprinted from* Technicalities, *v. 1, no. 1 (December 1980), pp. 6–7, by permission of M.E. Sharpe, Inc., Armonk NY 10504.*

## The Policy

In 1977, apparently responding to consumer demands for greater subject and title access, the Library of Congress publicly acknowledged that "often the concept of a work can be represented by a word or phrase occurring in its title," further noting that

> in most instances a heading which corresponds to this concept exists or can be established and assigned to the work. Sometimes, however, for new concepts it is impossible or impracticable to establish the concept and a broader heading or headings which represent the concept only approximately must be assigned. Whenever this occurs, the concept can still be made retrievable in the catalog either by the title added entry, or if the concept is not represented by the first words of the title proper, a partial title added entry.[6]

This tardy, but welcome, revelation triggered a four-point policy statement, highlighted by the instruction to "assign a partial title added entry when the subject heading assigned does not accurately represent the concept of the work and the concept is named or implied in the title proper but does not occur in the initial position."[7]

## The Practice

The need for generous title added entries has been firmly established in the literature. It has also been formally recognized by LC. And that ought to end the matter. But it doesn't, for actual practice suggests that the "new" policy is only applied fitfully and lamely by LC catalogers, and itself may be unduly constricted in scope. In evidence, here are a few recent and wholly typical examples of missed opportunities for expanding title-access:

Amoco Motor Club guide to mini-vacations in the Midwest.
MARC/CIP: No added entries.
Suggested: I. Title: Guide to mini-vacations in the Midwest. II. Title: Mini-vacations in the Midwest. III. Title: Midwest mini-vacations guide.

Crow, C.P.
No more Monday mornings.
MARC/CIP: I. Title.
Suggested: II. Title: Monday mornings.

Dupuy, Trevor N.
The almanac of world military power.
MARC/CIP: I. Title.
Suggested: II. Title. World military power almanac. III. Title: Military power almanac.

Fredman, Mike.
You can always blame the rain.
MARC/CIP: I. Title.
Suggested: II. Title: Blame the rain.

National Council of Teachers of English. Committee to Revise High Interest — Easy Reading.
High interest easy reading for junior and senior high school students.
MARC/CIP: I. Title.
Suggested: II. Title: Easy reading for junior and senior high school students.

Quirk, Randolph.
A concise grammar of contemporary English.
MARC/CIP: I. Title.
Suggested: II. Title: A grammar of contemporary English. III. Title: Contemporary English grammar.

Warring, Ronald Horace.
84 practical IC projects you can build.
MARC/CIP: I. Title.
Suggested: II. Title: Practical IC projects you can build. III. Title: IC projects you can build.

Bowers, Peter M.
A complete guide to aviation photography.
MARC/CIP: I. Title.
Suggested: II. Title: Aviation photography guide.

Lyons, Arthur.
Castles burning.
MARC/CIP: I. Title.
Suggested: II. Title: Burning castles.

Armstrong, William Howard, 1914- .
The tale of Tawny and Dingo.
MARC/CIP: I. Title.
Suggested: II. Title: Tawny and Dingo. III. Title: Dingo and Tawny.

The reasons for such delinquency may variously be oversight, an over-riding commitment to traditional praxis and parsimony, insufficient staff training, or ineffective quality control. Whatever the explanation, the practical outcome is that — except at the handful of libraries like OPL that deliberately and responsibly change outside copy to enhance access — catalog users remain *less* likely to find what they want, particularly since "most people do not persevere in catalog searches," more than 50% looking up only one entry and then stopping, "regardless of whether or not they have found what they are looking for."[8]

Heightened title-access represents a relatively inexpensive, yet proven way to improve "hit" rates *and* user-satisfaction. It therefore deserves special attention in cataloging codes (*AACR2* mandates no added entries for sub- or catch-titles),[9] urgent remedial action at the Library of Congress, and constant monitoring by local technical services staff.

## NOTES

1. "Catchwords, Subtitles, and Synthetic Subtitles," *Unabashed Librarian,* no. 1 (Nov. 1971): p. 32.
2. Ibid.
3. Pauline Atherton, "Catalog Users' Access from the Researcher's Viewpoint: Past and Present Research Which Could Affect Library Catalog Design," in *Closing the Catalog* (Phoenix: Oryx Press, 1980), p. 115.

4. Ibid., p. 107.

5. Ibid.

6. "Partial Title Added Entries," *Cataloging Service Bulletin,* no. 121 (Spring 1977): 16.

7. Ibid.

8. Atherton, p. 107.

9. See Rule 21.30J, p. 324. An additional rule has been recommended to correct this serious omission: "Trace Subtitles and Portions of Titles That Are Likely to Be Remembered and Sought." See S. Berman, "Proposed: *AACR2* Options and Addenda for School and Public Libraries," *Hennepin County Library Cataloging Bulletin,* no. 38 (Jan./Feb. 1979): 26. Also: Marvin H. Scilken, "The Catalog as a Public Service Tool," in *The Nature and Future of the Catalog* (Phoenix: Oryx Press, 1980), pp. 93–95; S. Berman, "Cataloging for Public Libraries," in *The Nature and Future of the Catalog,* p. 226; and Berman, "Getting to It," *Hennepin County Library Cataloging Bulletin,* no. 27 (April 1, 1977): 35.

# MISSING TITLES

A year after the call for more title added entries ("Title Access," *Technicalities,* vol. 1, no. 1, Dec. 1980, pp. 6–7), the situation hasn't changed much. If at all. For instance, LC traced solely the prime title of these recent books, making no added entries for obvious sub- or permuted titles:

| *Traced* | *Untraced* |
|---|---|
| Arabel and Mortimer | Mortimer and Arabel |
| Art of Biblical narrative | Biblical narrative art |
| Children of the Seventh Prophecy | Seventh Prophecy children |
| Comic adventures of Old Mother Hubbard and her dog | Old Mother Hubbard and her dog/ Mother Hubbard and her dog |
| Exit visa: the emigration of the Soviet Jews | Soviet Jews' emigration |
| Henrietta and the gong from Hong Kong | Gong from Hong Kong/Hong Kong gong |
| How and where to find gold: secrets of the '49ers | Secrets of the '49ers/'49ers' secrets |
| Legend of the Lone Ranger story-book | Lone Ranger storybook |
| McClane's North American fish cookery | North American fish cookery |
| Memoirs of an anti-Semite | Anti-Semite's memoirs |
| My diary — my world | My world — my diary |

*Reprinted from* Technicalities, *v. 2, no. 3 (March 1982), p. 11, by permission of M.E. Sharpe, Inc., Armonk NY 10504.*

| | |
|---|---|
| Never kiss a goat on the lips: the adventures of a suburban homesteader | Suburban homesteader's adventures |
| On the line: new gay fiction | Gay fiction/New gay fiction |
| Playfair: everybody's guide to noncompetitive play | Play fair: everybody's guide to noncompetitive play |
| Prayerways: for those who feel discouraged... | Prayer ways: for those who feel discouraged... |
| Prime time preachers: the rising power of televangelism | Televangelism's rising power |
| Prize stories of the seventies | Seventies' prize stories |
| Red earth, blue sky: the Australian Outback | Blue sky, red earth/Australian Outback/Outback |
| Smile...or I'll kick your bed! | I'll kick your bed! |
| Voyage of the jolly boat | Jolly boat voyage |

No problem, of course, in retrieving the "untraced" titles by means of online keyword or Boolean searching. But few libraries presently have the requisite hard- and software.

# THE TERRIBLE TRUTH ABOUT TEENLIT CATALOGING

The "TERRIBLE TRUTH" is simply this: Subject access to material by, for, and about teenagers is scandalously bad. This should come as no surprise to YA librarians and teens themselves. Surely they've known it for a long time. The "surprise" is that hardly anyone has raised hell about it.

The "scandal" divides nicely into two parts: vocabulary and heading assignment.

## Vocabulary

The source of teen-related subject headings for most libraries is the Library of Congress list (LCSH) or its abridged spin-off, Sears. And the threefold vocabulary problem is that LC (1) doesn't seem to know *what* to call teenagers and isn't at all consistent in terminology; (2) overwhelmingly favors "alien," clinical, "adult" nomenclature; and (3) doesn't contain nearly enough specific forms to reflect adequately the actual content of teen-related literature, whether novels, poetry, drama, or nonfiction.

To begin with the obvious: Teens don't call themselves "youth." They rarely refer to themselves as "adolescent" (indeed, that's a term of at least mild opprobrium, as in "Such *adolescent* behavior!"). They seldom think of one another as "YAs" or "young adults." And never as "juveniles." These are terms beloved by lawyers, psychologists, teachers, doctors, social workers, police, preachers, and yes, librarians, but *not* by teens. Nor do the mass media — magazines, newspapers, radio, TV, and films — ordinarily use such stuffy language. "Teen" (or "teenager") is *in*. In fact, it *has* been "in" for decades.

According to the December 1985 LCSH fiche, the Library of Congress list

*Reprinted from* Top of the News, *v. 43, no. 3 (Spring 1987), pp. 311–20, with permission of the American Library Association. "The Terrible Truth About Teenlit Cataloging" copyright © 1987 by ALA.*

boasts one solitary "teen" heading, albeit curiously hyphenated: TEEN-AGE MARRIAGE. This is how the whole entry looks:

Teen-age marriage
    sa  Adolescent mothers
         Pregnant schoolgirls
     x  Early marriage
   xx  Marriage
         Marriage age
         Pregnant schoolgirls
         Youth

The cross-references, intermixing both "adolescent" and "youth" rubrics, well illustrate the whole vocabulary muddle. Other "teen" entries that sensibly ought to be bona fide descriptors merely refer to a crazy-quilt of "adolescent," "juvenile," and "youth" forms:

Teen-age
  *See* Adolescence
Teen-age boys
  *See* Adolescent boys
Teen-age consumers
  *See* Youth as consumers
Teen-age drivers
  *See* Juvenile automobile drivers
Teen-age girls
  *See* Adolescent girls
Teen-age mothers
  *See* Adolescent mothers
Teen-age parents
  *See* Adolescent parents
Teen-age pregnancy
  *See* Pregnancy, Adolescent
Teen-age prostitution
  *See* Prostitution, Juvenile
Teen-agers
  *See* Youth

Two *see* references under YOUTH indicate that it's equivalent to "Adolescents" and "Teenagers," yet if YOUTH *really* denoted "adolescents" and "teenagers," why the already mentioned heading, TEEN-AGE MARRIAGE (instead of YOUTH MARRIAGE), and this roster of ADOLESCENT forms?:

Adolescent boys
Adolescent fathers [announced in LCSH weekly list no. 14, March 31, 1986]
Adolescent girls
Adolescent medicine
Adolescent mothers

Adolescent parents
Adolescent psychiatry
Adolescent psychology
Adolescent psychopathology
Adolescent psychotherapy

(Also, in practice, YOUTH often seems to be regarded as an umbrella term for one-to-twelve-year-olds *plus* teens.)

Further, what do YOUNG ADULTS and these related rubrics cover?:

Young adult drama
Young adult fiction
Young adult literature
Young adult poetry

(Probably "teenagers," together with drama, fiction, literature, and poetry for teens, but who knows for sure? Incidentally, Hennepin County Library also employs "Young adults," but clarifies in a scope-note that it applies strictly to "persons 18 to 25 years old.")

In fairness, there *are* more "youth" headings than any other kind; e.g.:

Youth, Afro-American [Bahai, Hindu, etc.]
Youth and death
Youth and erotica
Youth and mass media
Youth centers
Youth in art [television, etc.]
Youth sermons
Youth travel
Youth's periodicals
Youth's writings

And even two doubly undesirable forms, YOUTH AS ARTISTS and YOUTH AS CONSUMERS, which not only aren't clear about what age group's involved, but also manage to slander whatever bracket's intended by implying that their age alone renders them unlikely artists or consumers.

In short, LCSH's teen-related language doesn't reflect "real," everyday usage, and is massively confused and inconsistent in both scope and form, needlessly dispersing "teen" material throughout the catalog and grossly inhibiting first-hit searches.

The third vocabulary problem—that of insufficient headings—is best demonstrated by examining honest-to-God heading assignments.

## Heading Assignment

The trouble here is that even the available, if shoddy, vocabulary isn't always applied when it should be; many works demand more (and frequently more specific) subject tracings than they get; the assigned headings often ignore the age dimension, thus frustrating direct access to the "teen" element; and LC catalogers sometimes miss the chance to make or amplify notes that might help potential readers or users decide whether a given work is really what they want. Examples of LC/MARC and Hennepin County Library records are listed in appendix A.

## What to Do?

If teenlit cataloging is so miserably mucked up, what can be done about it? Two things:

1. Critically examine and revise teenlit records in-house or at the network level; and

2. Lobby the ALA Cataloging of Children's Materials Committee and Library of Congress Children's Literature Cataloging Section to rationalize and modernize LCSH vocabulary and better analyze teen-related works.

## Appendix A: Examples of LC Marc and Hennepin County Library Records

### LC/MARC Record

Coles, Robert.
  Sex and the American teenager. 1985.
  "An American [sic!] undercover special on HBO." — Cover.
  1. Youth — United States — Sexual behavior.

### Hennepin County Library (HCL) Record

Coles, Robert.
  Sex and the American teenager. 1985.
  "An America undercover special on HBO."
  "Based on a survey of 1,067 respondents."
  PARTIAL CONTENTS: A psychological perspective. –Social profile. –Sources of sexual information: how they learn. –Logistics: where and when and how much. –Intimacy: how they express it. Virginity: keeping it and losing it. Parents: letting them know. Going steady/breaking up. Rape, casual sex, group sex. Birth control, pregnancy, and abortion. Homosexuality. –Interviews.
  APPENDIX: The questionnaire.

1. Teenagers — Sexuality.   2.
Teenagers — United States — Inter-
views.      3. Teenagers — United
States — Attitudes. 4. Teenagers —
Birth control. 5. Teenagers —
United States — Lifestyles.

Brower, Millicent.
Young performers on the stage, in
film, and on TV. 1985.
SUMMARY: Presents profiles of
Matthew Broderick, Sarah Jessica
Parker, and six other young actors
and actresses, ranging in age from
thirteen to twenty-three.
1. Entertainers — United States —
Biography. 2. Children as actors —
United States. 3. Children as ac-
tors. 4. Actors and actresses.

Brower, Millicent.
Young performers on the stage, in
film, and on TV. 1985.
SUMMARY: Presents profiles of
Matthew Broderick, Sarah Jessica
Parker, and six other young actors
ranging in age from thirteen to
twenty-three. Includes glossary.
1. Entertainers, American. 2.
Teenage film actors and actresses. 3.
Teenage television actors and ac-
tresses. 4. Actors and actresses,
American. 5. Broderick, Matthew.
6. Parker, Sarah Jessica.

Korman, Gordon.
Don't Care High. 1985.
SUMMARY: Paul's attempts to ad-
just to New York City life are
thwarted at his high school, nick-
named Don't Care High, until his
manipulation of a new Student
Council president wakes up the apa-
thetic student body.
1. High schools — Fiction. 2.
Schools — Fiction. 3. New York
(N.Y.) — Fiction.

Korman, Gordon.
Don't Care High. 1985.
SUMMARY: Paul's attempts to ad-
just to New York City life are
thwarted at his high school, nick-
named Don't Care High, until his
manipulation of a new Student
Council president wakes up the apa-
thetic student body.
1. High schools — New York City
— Fiction. 2. Teenage boys — New
York City — Fiction. 3. Apathy in
teenagers — Fiction. 4. High school
sophomores — New York City —
Fiction. 5. Manipulation (Social
sciences) — Fiction.    6. Student
government — Fiction.    7. New
York City — Fiction.

Lee, Rose P.
A real job for you: an employ-
ment guide for teens. 1985.
SUMMARY: An employment

Lee, Rose P.
A real job for you: an employ-
ment guide for teens. 1985.
SUMMARY: An employment

guide for teenagers looking for their first job, covering social security cards, references, resumes, interviews, and other subjects.

1. Vocational guidance.

guide for teenagers looking for their first job, covering social security cards, references, resumes, interviews, and other subjects.

1. Vocational guidance for teengers. 2. Job hunting for teenagers. 3. First job.

Stolz, Mary.
The explorer of Barkham Street. 1985.

SUMMARY: Reformed bully Martin Hastings fantasizes about heroic adventures as an explorer and a sports star, until his new friends and growing self-confidence at home make real life as exciting as his daydreams.

1. Children's stories, American. 2. Self-acceptance — Fiction. 3. Imagination — Fiction. 4. Family life — Fiction.

Stolz, Mary.
The explorer of Barkham Street. 1985.

SUMMARY: Reformed bully Martin Hastings fantasizes about heroic adventures as an explorer and a sports star, until his new friends and growing self-confidence at home make real life as exciting as his daydreams.

1. Daydreams — Fiction. 2. Self-acceptance in teenagers — Fiction. 3. Imagination in teenagers — Fiction. 4. Family problems — Fiction. 5. Thirteen-year-old boys — Fiction. 6. Teenage boys — Interpersonal relations — Fiction.

Murphy, Shirley Rousseau.
Nightpool. 1985.

SUMMARY: Injured in battle with the Dark Raiders, sixteen-year-old Tebriel is healed by a colony of talking otters and sets out to fight the Dark and its forces of evil in the world of Tirror.

1. Fantasy.

Murphy, Shirley Rousseau.
Nightpool. 1985.

SUMMARY: Injured in battle with the Dark Raiders, sixteen-year-old Tebriel is healed by a colony of talking otters and sets out to fight the Dark and its forces of evil in the world of Tirror.

1. Fantasy fiction, American. 2. Sixteen-year-old boys — Fiction. 3. Teenage heroes and heroines — Fiction. 4. Good and evil — Fiction.

Stren, Patti.
I was a 15-year-old blimpo. 1985.

SUMMARY: Fifteen-year-old Gabby resorts to drastic measures in her struggle to lose weight but finds there is more to being grown up

Stren, Patti.
I was a 15-year-old blimpo. 1985.

SUMMARY: Fifteen-year-old Gabby resorts to drastic measures in her struggle to lose weight but finds there is more to being grown up than being skinny.

1. Weight control — Fiction. 2. Bulimarexia — Fiction. 3. Mothers and daughters — Fiction. 4. Interpersonal relations — Fiction.

than being skinny.

1. Fifteen-year-old girls — Fiction. 2. Overweight teenagers — Fiction. 3. Weight control for teenage girls — Fiction. 4. Bulimia — Fiction. 5. Mother and daughter — Fiction. 6. Teenage girls — Interpersonal relations — Fiction. 7. Weight loss camps — Fiction. 8. Self-acceptance in teenagers — Fiction. 9. Looksism — Fiction.

Landau, Elaine.

Different drummer: homosexuality in America. 1986.

SUMMARY: Discusses the emotional, social, and physical aspects of homosexuality and the problems encountered by homosexuals and lesbians in an anti-homosexual society.

1. Homosexuality.

Landau, Elaine.

Different drummer: homosexuality in America. 1986.

SUMMARY: Discussions and interviews with gay and lesbian teens cover a wide range of lifestyles, and there is information about mental health and the law, as well as suggestions for gay and lesbian teenagers concerned with informing their family members.

PARTIAL CONTENTS: Roots of homophobia. -AIDS crisis. -Bibliography.

1. Homophobia — United States. 2. Gay teenagers. 3. Gay teenagers — Interviews. 4. Gay teenagers — Family relationships. 5. Lesbian teenagers. 6. Lesbian teenagers — Interviews. 7. Lesbian teenagers — Family relationships. 8. AIDS.

Shaw, Diana.

Make the most of a good thing: you! 1985.

SUMMARY: Offers the adolescent girl advice on sexual changes in the body, diet and nourishment, exercise, dealing with stress, and staying healthy.

1. Adolescent girls — Health and hygiene. 2. Health.

Shaw, Diana.

Make the most of a good thing: you! 1985.

Jacket subtitle: What you need to know about exercise, diet, stress, sexuality, relationships, and more.

SUMMARY: Offers teenage girls advice on sexual change in the body, diet and nourishment, exercise, dealing with stress, and staying healthy.

1. Teenage girls — Health. 2. Teenage girls — Nutrition. 3. Teenage girls — Sexuality. 4. Exercise for teenage girls. 5. Teenage girls — Stress.

Weston, Carol.

Girltalk: all the stuff your sister never told you. 1985.

1. Adolescent girls. 2. Adolescent girls — Conduct of life.

Weston, Carol.

Girltalk: all the stuff your sister never told you. 1985.

PARTIAL CONTENTS: Body: looking and feeling your best. -Friendship. -Love: falling in, falling out. -Sex: what you should know before saying yes. -Family: can't live with 'em, can't live without 'em. -Money: the buck starts here. -Drinks, drugs, etc.

1. Teenage girls. 2. Beauty care for teenage girls. 3. Teenage girls — Friendship. 4. Teenage girls — Sexuality. 5. Teenage girls — Drug use. 6. Teenage girls — Family relationships. 7. Teenage girls — Personal conduct. 8. Teenage romance. 9. Teenage girls — Personal finance.

Richmond, Sandra.

Wheels for walking. 1983.

SUMMARY: After a car accident severs her spinal cord, eighteen-year-old Sally faces a long and painful adjustment to life as a quadriplegic.

1. Quadriplegics — Fiction. 2. Physically handicapped — Fiction.

Richmond, Sandra.

Wheels for walking. 1983.

SUMMARY: After a car accident severs her spinal cord, eighteen-year-old Sally faces a long and painful adjustment to life as a quadriplegic.

1. Teenage quadriplegics — Fiction. 2. Physically disabled teenagers — Fiction. 3. Eighteen-year-old girls — Fiction. 4. Wheelchair users — Fiction. 5. Teenage romance — Fiction. 6. Spinal cord — Wounds and injuries — Fiction.

Guy, David.

Second brother. 1985.

Guy, David.

Second brother. 1985.

1. Pittsburgh — Fiction. 2. The

Sixties — Fiction. 3. Coming-of-age stories. 4. Sibling rivalry — Fiction. 5. Brothers — Pittsburgh — Fiction. 6. Teenage boys — Friendship — Fiction. 7. Teenagers — Pittsburgh — Fiction.

Forshay-Lunsford, Cin.
Walk through cold fire. 1985.
SUMMARY: A sixteen-year-old girl with a miserable home life finds love and friendship for one heartbreaking summer with a gang of other teenagers with problems.
1. Identity (Psychology) — Fiction. 2. Teenage rebels — Fiction. 3. Gangs — Fiction. 4. Middle class — United States — Fiction. 5. Sixteen-year-old girls — Fiction. 6. Teenagers and death — Fiction. 7. Teenage romance — Fiction. 8. Teenagers — Family relationships — Fiction. 9. Teenagers — Friendship — Fiction.

Highsmith, Patricia.
People who knock at the door. 1985.
1. "Born again" Christians — Fiction. 2. Brothers — Fiction. 3. Small town families — Fiction. 4. Mother and son — Fiction. 5. Father and son — Fiction. 6. Extramarital relations — Fiction. 7. Teenage boys — Fiction. 8. Patricide — Fiction. 9. High school seniors — Fiction. 10. Fifteen-year-old boys — Fiction. 11. Teenage abortion — Fiction. 12. Religious fanaticism — Fiction. 13. Christian fundamentalists — Fiction. 14. Miracles (Christianity) — Fiction. 15. Hypocrisy — Fiction.

Adams, Caren.

No is not enough: helping teenagers avoid sexual assault. 1984.

1. Sex instruction. 2. Rape—Prevention. 3. Youth—Crimes against.

No is not enough: helping teenagers avoid sexual assault. 1984.

PARTIAL CONTENTS: Acquaintance rape and sexual exploitation. -Self-esteem: a tool for protection. -Just friends: overcoming sex role expectations. -Touch: affection, confusion, exploitation. -Uses and misuses of sex. -Family stress: more risk for teens. -Recovery: responding if your teen is assaulted.

1. Sex education for teenagers. 2. Teenage sexual abuse—Prevention. 3. Rape of teenage girls—Prevention. 4. Teenagers—Sexuality. 5. Self-esteem in teenage girls. 6. Teenage girls—Interpersonal relations. 7. Teenage rape victims—Treatment. 8. Teenage girls—Development and guidance. 9. Date rape.

## Appendix B: Recent HCL Subject Heading Innovations, A Selection*

Apathy in teenagers.
cn Assignment (with —NEW YORK CITY—FICTION): Gordon Korman's *Don't Care High* (1985).
sf Apathy, Teenage
 Teen apathy
 Teenage apathy
 Teenagers' apathy
xx Teenagers
 Teenagers—Psychology

Autistic teenagers.
cn Assignment: Eric Schopler and Gary B. Mesibov's *Autism in adolescents and adults* (1983).

sf Teenagers, Autistic
xx Autistic children
 Autistic persons
 Learning disabled teenagers

Beauty care for teenage girls.
cn Assignment (with —PERIODICALS): *YM: young miss magazine.*
sa Grooming for teenage girls
sf Teen beauty care
 Teenage beauty care
 Teenage girls—Beauty care
 Teenagers' beauty care
xx Grooming for teenage girls
 Teenage girls

*cn = cataloger's note; pn = public note; sa = see also; sf = see from; xx = see also from.

Exercise for teenagers.
cn Assignment: Bruce Jenner's *Athletic body: a complete fitness guide for teenagers — sports, strength, health, agility* (1984)
sa Weight training for teenagers
sf Teen exercise
Teenage exercise
Teenagers — Exercise
xx Exercise for children
Physical fitness for teenagers
Teenagers — Health

Funk music.
cn Authority: David Bianco, "Glossary of new wave musical terms," in his *Who's new wave in music* (1985), p. 356. Assignment: Bar-Kays' *Banging the wall* (1985 LP); Con Funk Shun's *Electric lady* (1985 LP); Funkadelic's *Hardcore jollies* (1976 LP).
pn Here is entered "soul-oriented dance music, usually with a complex rhythmic beat" [source: Bianco].
sf Funky music
Music, Funk
xx Soul music

Job hunting for teenage girls.
cn Assignment: Catalyst, Inc.'s *It's your future! Catalyst's career guide for high school girls* (1984).
sf Teenage girls' job hunting
xx Job hunting for teenagers
Job hunting for women
Teenage girls — Employment
Vocational guidance for teenage girls

Preteens.
cn Authority: *Thesaurus of ERIC descriptors* (1984), p. 199; PREADOLESCENTS. Assignment: Hershel

D. Thornberg's *Bubblegum years: sticking with kids from 9–13* (1983).
pn Here are entered materials on persons 9–12 years of age [source: ERIC].
sa Eleven-year-olds
Nine-year-olds
Ten-year-olds
Twelve-year-olds
sf Adolescents, Pre
Preadolescents
Teenagers, Pre
Teens, Pre
xx Children
Eleven-year-olds
Nine-year-olds
Teenagers
Ten-year-olds
Twelve-year-olds

Teenage abortion.
cn Assignment: Elizabeth R. McAnanarney's *Premature adolescent pregnancy and parenthood* (1983), which includes "Abortion in adolescence."
sf Abortion, Teenage
Adolescent abortion
Teen abortion
Teenage girls — Abortion
Teenager abortion
xx Abortion
Teenage pregnancy

Teenage ballet dancers.
cn Assignment: Alexandra Collard's *Two young dancers: their world of ballet* (1984).
sf Ballet dancers, Teenage
Teen ballet dancers
xx Ballet dancers
Child ballet dancers

Teenage cancer patients.
cn Assignment (with — PERSONAL

NARRATIVES): Carol Simonides'
*I'll never walk alone: the inspiring*
*story of a teenager's struggle against*
*cancer* (1983).
sf Cancer patients, Teenage
   Teen cancer patients
xx Cancer patients
   Child cancer patients
   Teenagers—Health

Teenage explorers.
cn Assignment (with —THE WEST
   [UNITED STATES]—FICTION):
   Charles Bohner's *Bold journey:*
   *West with Lewis and Clark* (1985).
sf Explorers, Teenage
   Teen explorers
xx Explorers
   Teenage adventurers

Teenage incest victims.
cn Assignment (with —FICTION):
   Patricia Hermes' *Solitary secret*
   (1985).
sf Incest victims, Teenage
   Teen incest victims
xx Incest victims
   Teenage girls
   Teenage rape victims

Teenage rape victims.
cn Assignment (with —LONGITU-
   DINAL STUDIES): Suzanne S.
   Ageton's *Sexual assault among ado-*
   *lescents* (1983).
sf Adolescent rape victims
   Rape victims, Teenage
   Teen rape victims
xx Rape victims
   Teenage girls

Teenage rapists.
cn Assignment (with —LONGITUD-
   INAL STUDIES): Suzanne S. Ageton's *Sexual assault among adoles-*
   *cents* (1983).

sf Adolescent rapists
   Rapists, Teenage
   Teen rapists
xx Rapists
   Teenage boys
   Teenage sex offenders

Teenage sexual abuse.
cn Class in 362.71. Assignment:
   Ruth S. and C. Henry Kempe's
   *Common secret: sexual abuse of*
   *children and adolescents* (1984).
sa Child sexual abuse
sf Sexual abuse, Teenage
   Teen sexual abuse
   Teenager sexual abuse
   Teenagers' sexual abuse
xx Child sexual abuse
   Teenage abuse

Teenage shoplifters.
cn Assignment (with —FICTION):
   C.S. Adler's *With Westie and the*
   *Tin Man* (1985).
sf Shoplifters, Teenage
   Teen shoplifters
xx Juvenile delinquents
   Shoplifting

Teenage television actors and actresses.
cn Assignment (with —FICTION):
   Karen Rose and Lynda Half-
   yard's *Kristin and Boone* (1983).
sf Teen television actors and actresses
   Television actors and actresses,
   Teenage
xx Teenage actors and actresses
   Television actors and actresses

Teenagers and computers.
cn Assignment (with —FICTION):
   Sandy Landsman's *Gadget factor*
   (1984).

sf  Computers and teenagers
    Teenagers — Computer use
xx  Children and computers
    Computers

Teenagers' letters.
cn  Assignment: Judy Blume's *Letters to Judy: what your kids wish they could tell you* (1986)
sf  Letters, Teenagers'
    Teen letters
xx  Letters
    Teenagers' writings

Teenagers — Stress.
cn  Previous HCL form: STRESS IN TEENAGERS.
sf  Stress in teenagers

    Teen stress
    Teenage stress
xx  Stress
    Teenagers — Mental health
    Teenagers — Psychology

Wet dreams.
cn  Assignment: Gail Jones Sanchez and Mary Gerbino's *Let's talk about sex and loving* (1983), which includes "What are wet dreams?"
sf  Dreams, Wet
    Nocturnal emissions
xx  Dreams
    Men — Sexuality
    Orgasm
    Teenage boys — Sexuality

# C'MON, GUYS, LIGHTEN UP!

Last year Little, Brown published Carol McD. Wallace's *Should You Shut Your Eyes When You Kiss? Or, How to Survive "The Best Years of Your Life."* The teen-targeted work cheerfully recommends how to avoid school, "how to survive a family vacation," and "how to look taller than you are." On page 19, Wallace offers this advice on such "respectable dirty books" as *Ulysses, Tropic of Capricorn,* and *Lady Chatterley's Lover:*

> If you want to take them out, be careful; otherwise the librarian and your parents will know exactly why you wanted to read them. You can try to camouflage the key titles by checking them out along with other books. If, for instance, the author has written anything else, select two or three extra volumes so the librarian merely thinks you're a D.H. Lawrence buff. Or add a biography or critical study so you look like a young Joyce scholar. At home, keep the *interesting* book in the middle of the stack, and your parents may overlook it completely.

And on page 69, under a "First Bra" banner, appears this (typical) admonition:

> Even if you don't really need a bra, you should have one so that you have something to stuff.

Well, whether sophomoric, vulgar, or screamingly funny, what Wallace's book *isn't* is serious. Yet DCD soberly put it in 646.70088055 (that's in the "Management of Personal and Family Living" schedule), a stunning case of classificatory overkill, and apparently humorless SCDers subject cataloged it thusly:

1. Youth—Life skills guides.
2. Students—Life skills guides.
3. Youth—Family relationships.

At HCL, we smirkingly classified it 817.54 (contemporary American humor), and composed this annotation:

> SUMMARY: Tongue-in-cheek advice to teenagers on such topics as homework, dating, sex, grooming, and driving.

*Reprinted from* Technicalities, *v. 4, no. 12 (December 1984), p. 9, by permission of M.E. Sharpe, Inc., Armonk NY 10504.*

and supplied seven subject tracings:

1. American humor—20th century.
2. Teenagers—Life skills guides—Parodies.
3. Teenagers—Humor.
4. Students—Life skills guides—Parodies.
5. Teenagers—Lifestyles—Humor.
6. Teenagers—Sexuality—Humor.
7. Teenagers—Family relationships—Humor.

# CATALOG ACCESS
# TO CONSUMER
# HEALTH INFORMATION

Assuming the public's right to health information, including "nontraditional" and "alternative" materials, and believing that access to data should be as quick and painless as possible, at least four problem areas in current subject cataloging practice need immediate attention and reform:

1. A frequently awkward, technical, clinical vocabulary that frustrates "first-try hits" by lay users. In these examples, the commonly used health terms are followed by headings which have been assigned by LC.

Smoking hazards/Smoking and health: TOBACCO — PHYSIOLOGICAL EFFECT

Anticancer drugs: ANTINEOPLASTIC AGENTS

PCP/"Angel dust": PHENCYCLIDINE

PBBs: POLYBROMINATED BIPHENYLS

PCBs: POLYCHLORINATED BIPHENYLS

Child care/Child health: CHILDREN — CARE AND HYGIENE

Birth defects: ABNORMALITIES, HUMAN

Tay-Sachs Disease: AMAUROTIC FAMILY IDIOCY

Menstrual cramps: DYSMENORRHEA

2. Missing vocabulary: topics amply represented in the literature but not yet recognized nor sanctioned in standard subject heading schemes and thesauri.

Examples:

HEALTH HAZARDS [as a subhead, e.g., under ASBESTOS, HOUSES, INDUSTRIAL CHEMICALS, PLUTONIUM, SCHOOL BUILDINGS, etc.]

MEDICAID SERVICES

*Reprinted from* Technicalities, *v. 2, no. 1 (January 1982), pp. 6–7, by permission of M.E. Sharpe, Inc., Armonk NY 10504.*

MEDICARE SERVICES

HEALTH — HANDBOOKS, MANUALS, ETC. (FOR SOUTHEAST ASIAN REFUGEES)

FAMILY PLANNING [*not* identical to BIRTH CONTROL]

FAMILY PLANNING SERVICES

VOCATIONAL REHABILITATION CENTERS

OCCUPATIONAL REPRODUCTIVE HAZARDS

HOSPITAL CHOICE

NURSING HOME REFORM

POLARITY THERAPY

GAMBLING ADDICTION

BATES METHOD

CRABS (DISEASE)

CHILD NEGLECT [*not* synonymous with "Child abuse"]

CHILD PROTECTIVE SERVICES

ADULT PROTECTION SERVICES

DISABILITY RIGHTS MOVEMENT

HOME SAFETY

GENERIC DRUGS

INVOLUNTARY TREATMENT (OF PRISONERS, MENTAL PATIENTS, ETC.)

ELDER ABUSE

LIVING WILL

NESTLE BOYCOTT

SEX MANUALS

TUBAL LIGATION

ALTERNATIVE FUNERALS

BATTERED WOMEN [nearest LCSH rubric: ABUSED WIVES]

CERVICAL CAP (BIRTH CONTROL)

PREGNANCY COUNSELING

PREGNANCY TESTING

SPONGE (BIRTH CONTROL)

SEX-CHANGE SURGERY

WORKAHOLISM

PATIENTS' RIGHTS [nearest LCSH rubric: HOSPITAL PATIENTS — LEGAL STATUS, LAWS, ETC.]

MENTAL PATIENTS' LIBERATION MOVEMENT

NATIONAL HEALTH INSURANCE

STERILIZATION OF POOR AND MINORITY WOMEN

FAMILY PROTECTION ACT (PROPOSED)

HUMAN LIFE AMENDMENT (PROPOSED)

HUMAN LIFE STATUTE (PROPOSED)

3. Inadequate cross-referencing from unused, but likely-to-be-sought, equivalents; e.g.,

Acupuncture
  x Accupuncture
Prostate gland
  x Prostrate gland
Prostate gland — Cancer
  x Cancer of the prostate
Rheumatism
  x Reumatism
    Roomatism
I.U.D.
  x Barrier methods (Birth control)
    Intrauterine device

PCP
  x "Amoeba" (Drug)
    "Angel dust" (Drug)
    "CJ" (Drug)
    "Cadillac" (Drug)
    "Cyclones" (Drug)
    "Mist" (Drug)
    "Peace pills" (Drug)
    Phencyclidine
    "Rocket fuel" (Drug)
    "Scuffle" (Drug)
    "Supergrass" (Drug)

4. Miserly heading assignment and failure to make subject analytics for significant portions or aspects of larger works. For instance, LC assigned to Richard Rashke's *Killing of Karen Silkwood* (Houghton Mifflin, 1981) no heading comparable to NUCLEAR POWER INDUSTRY WORKERS — HEALTH; Jo Roman's *Exit House* (Seaview Books, 1980), which deals with "choosing suicide as an alternative," got only the somewhat bizarre SUICIDE — BIOGRAPHY, no RIGHT TO DIE nor CANCER PATIENTS — PERSONAL NARRATIVES; Norman Cousins' *Anatomy of an Illness as Perceived by the Patient* (1979) warranted, but didn't receive, a tracing for HUMOR — THERAPEUTIC USE; and John L. Marshall's *Sports Doctor's Fitness Book for Women* (Delacorte, 1981), containing chapters on "Your Medical Profile" and "Fitness Facilities and How to Rate Them," merited helpful analytics like HEALTH PROFILING and HEALTH CLUBS — EVALUATION.

If these are the maladies, what's the medicine? For starters:

• Lobby the cataloging and indexing providers — such as LC and the National Library of Medicine — to be more user-sensitive, contemporary in language, and alert to new topics.

• As resources permit, perform in-house "tinkering" to make vital information more accessible to local patrons: freely create new headings and modernize old ones, generously add "see" and "see also" references, and perhaps introduce I & R-type notes under appropriate subject descriptors (e.g., "ADULT PROTECTION SERVICES — RANDOLPH COUNTY, FLORIDA. For more information on Randolph County adult protection services, phone 731-4980").

And nonlibrarian consumers should firmly demand improved "findability" from librarians and other information suppliers, letting them know *what* they want and *how* they expect to locate it. These are, after all, literally matters of life and death.

# ORWELLIAN POSTSCRIPT TO THE PROPOSED SUBHEAD "—HEALTH HAZARDS"

According to the December 1981 *Statewatch* (Minnesota Public Interest Research Group), the Environmental Protection Agency last year "won" a National Council of Teachers of English Doublespeak Award because:

John Hernandez, deputy administrator of EPA, explained that words like "hazard" will not be used and instead of talking about "degree of hazard," the EPA will talk about "degree of mitigation of risk." The Office of Hazardous Emergency Response has been renamed the Office of Emergency and Remedial Response, while EPA enforcement personnel will now be called compliance assistance officers. The agency will also avoid the word "cancer-causing".... Thus, the EPA recently decided not to publicize new findings that certain wood preservatives might cause cancer, as well as no longer identifying toxic chemicals that have been found to cause genetic abnormalities or birth defects.... An EPA press aide [said] that "It might scare too many people."

Incidentally, Hennepin County Library has already assigned the—HEALTH HAZARDS subdivision to at least 115 primary subject headings, among them ALCOHOL, AMMONIA, ASBESTOS, COFFEE, COMPUTER TERMINALS, COTTON DUST, ESTROGEN, FIBERGLASS, FORMALDEHYDE, MICROWAVES, OFFICES, RADIATION, SCHOOL BUILDINGS, SHIFT WORK, SMOKING, and X-RAYS. Further, HCL routinely applies the descriptor, CARCINOGENS (cross-referenced from "Cancer-causing agents"), whenever it fits the material being cataloged, such as *Toxic Chemicals and Public Protection* (GPO, 1980), which includes a section on "Cancers and Carcinogens: A Prevention Policy."

*Reprinted from* Technicalities, *v. 2, no. 2 (February 1982), p. 7, by permission of M.E. Sharpe, Inc., Armonk NY 10514.*

# THANKS A LOT!

It should have been easy. A major reference-book publisher (Facts On File). "Library of Congress Cataloging in Publication Data" on the title page verso. Something a clerk could easily handle. A splendid example of how national standards and centralized cataloging save time and money. Except it wasn't.

This is the CIP entry for John Tepper Marlin and James S. Avery's 1983 volume, *The Book of American City Rankings:*

```
Main entry under title:

Marlin, John Tepper.
    The Book of American City Rankings.

    Includes index.
    1. Cities and towns — United States — Handbooks,
manuals, etc. I. James S. Avery
    HT123.B64        306'.0973        82-2437
    ISBN 0-87196-685-9          AACR2
```

Although specifying "main entry under title," the CIP record itself main-entered the work under the first-named of the two joint authors, "Marlin." Then, perhaps operating on the premise that the book was, in fact, a title main entry, the tracings showed no

    I. Title.

And while the second author, "Avery," got an appropriate added entry, his name appears in uninverted form, making it unuseable — i.e., unfindable — in library catalogs. Further, even though a) "American City Rankings" appears on the title page in dramatically bold type, b) "City rankings" would be an ideal proto-subject approach to the content, and c) both the t.p. verso

*Reprinted from* Technicalities, *v. 4, no. 3 (March 1984), pp. 6, 16, by permission of M.E. Sharpe, Inc., Armonk NY 10504.*

and "front matter" clearly associate the authors and their product with COMP, the Council on Municipal Performance, the LC/CIP treatment mandated no such access points, i.e., no

II. Council on Municipal Performance.

III. Title: American city rankings.

IV. Title: City rankings.

In sum, the in-book CIP record: makes it unclear whether to enter the work under title or personal author; renders the joint author and COMP inaccessible; and if accepted "as is," probably would result in *no* title-access whatever.

# INDOOR FLINGS

Question: What number did LC's Dewey classifiers assign to Emily Ann Donaldson's *Scottish Highland Games in America* (1986)? Answer: 793.02573. Question: So what's so awful about that? Answer: "793" denotes "indoor games and amusements," while the "02573" represents an "American directory." But the directory, titled "Listings of games in the United States," only occupies a small portion of the whole book. And "Highland Games," whether held in Scotland or America, invariably take place *out*side, which the numerous photos in Donaldson's tome clearly indicate. Question: Didn't the LC classifiers *see* the whole book, including those tell-tale photos? Answer: Maybe not, particularly if all they worked from was a CIP form without even any "front matter." Question: If LC classifiers and catalogers frequently handle just pieces of paper instead of real, finished books (or at least complete galleys), couldn't that adversely affect the quality and accuracy of LC/MARC records? Answer: Probably. In fact, one LC Division Chief lately admitted in a reply to someone who had questioned the treatment of a particular title that "when this work came through as a CIP, we may not have had sufficient information to analyze it correctly."

*Reprinted from* Technicalities, *v. 7, no. 5 (May 1987), p. 7, by permission of M.E. Sharpe, Inc., Armonk NY 10504.*

# INDOOR FLINGS
# (CONTINUED)

Question: How did LC classify and subject catalog James J. Kavanaugh's *From Loneliness To Love* (Harper & Row, 1986)?

Answer: It got a 302.545 Dewey number and three subject tracings: 1. Social isolation. 2. Loneliness. 3. Love.

Q: Judging from the title, that's not bad. What's the gripe? A: Simply that it's not a social science work. Not primarily, anyway. It's poetry. Q: Poetry?! A: Yes, poetry. Free verse. It starts on page 10 and keeps going. *Any*body can see that's it's verse, not prose. Q: How come, then, that the LC catalogers didn't see it? A: Possibly for the same reason that they didn't see that whole Highland Games book, which would have made it graphically obvious that the Games take place outdoors and that the book itself was *not* mainly or even largely a "directory." In short, they probably cataloged both titles from CIP forms alone, certainly not from full galleys and apparently without even much "front matter" or actual page samples.

Q: So examining the whole—or even part—of Kavanaugh's volume would have produced a more reliable, accurate cataloging record? A: Absolutely. Seeing the text *in verse* would doubtless have resulted in a correct "literature" notation—like 811.54 for contemporary American poetry. But even though Kavanaugh *does* deal—poetically—with those three topics of "Social isolation," "Loneliness," and "Love," the likelihood is that none of them would have been assigned as subject headings to the *poetry book* because LC's policy is *not* to apply either topical or genre headings to single-author literary works. The volume, in short, would certainly have been better classified, but in the process would also have lost *all* subject access.

Q: There *must* be a way to avoid this kind of situation, right? A: There are two ways, both involving major policy changes. First, the CIP process needs to be reexamined and revamped to ensure that *every* CIP title is, in fact, cataloged on the basis of sufficient information. And if it proves impossible

*Reprinted from* Technicalities, *v. 7, no. 6 (June 1987), pp. 12, 14, by permission of M.E. Sharpe, Inc., Armonk NY 10504.*

to secure "sufficient information" for most CIP items, then — drastic as it may sound — the program should be dropped and the resources previously devoted to it redirected to the timely and credible cataloging of *published* works. Second, LC's current policy of assigning appropriate genre and topical headings solely to literary *collections* should be expanded to include single-authored works. The happy consequence of both policy changes is that Kavanaugh's book — as a prototypical example — would be correctly classified (and shelved) in the 800s *and* would be found in the catalog under SOCIAL ISOLATION — POETRY, LONELINESS — POETRY, LOVE — POETRY, and AMERICAN POETRY — 20TH CENTURY.

# CENSORSHIP/
# HUMAN RIGHTS

# NOTES FROM EUROPE

*Freiburg, 11 July 1967*

*Stuttgart, sometime in March.* In a lecture on the role of Amerika Häuser in Germany, the local USIS Director enunciated an interesting "mainstream theory" of book selection. He was proud, he said, that Amerika Haus libraries do *not* furnish *Howl, Last Exit to Brooklyn, Tropic of Cancer, Naked Lunch, Dissent, Evergreen Review, American Opinion, The Dutchman, Church and State, Another Country, Ramparts, The Realist, Candy,* W.E.B. DuBois, Jules Feiffer, Nat Hentoff, Norman Thomas, *In White America,* Zinn's *SNCC,* Nazi-Chief Rockwell, *Liberation, Human Events, Suicide of the West, Accidental Century, Presidential Papers, Malcolm X Speaks,* Dwight MacDonald's *Against the American Grain, Air-Conditioned Nightmare* or Paul Goodman. He hoped they never would. Such books, periodicals, and writers are unrepresentative, outside the "mainstream." By implication, they are not quite "American." By no means does such a policy qualify as "censorship," he held, slightly offended at the suggestion. After all, the library has Fulbright's newest volume, Goldwater's *Conscience of a Conservative,* Eisenhower's *Memoirs,* and subscribes to *The Reporter!* Oh, rapture! Oh, nuts!

I believe and want to underscore that the problem of USIS policy is most serious, for the present "mainstream" stance betrays a stiflingly conformist, illiberal, regressive — yes, basically totalitarian — philosophy. It surely does not square with the "Library Bill of Rights" and can hardly promote much respect for us among literate folk abroad. It is from variety and ferment that both our strength and vitality spring.

*Athens, 21-29 April.* Strange to spend a first night in the "cradle of democracy" jarred from sleep — three hours long — by staccato bursts from automatic weapons. Trigger-happy juvenile delinquents in Greek Army uniforms — American equipped — roam the empty streets. Tanks and half-tracks blockade the center of town. Ten machine guns have sprouted atop the Parliament Building. Steel hatted troops swarm over the Olympic Stadium. Small cannon pivot below the whitewashed Byzantine chapel on Lykabettus

*Reprinted with permission from* Newsletter on Intellectual Freedom, *v. 16, no. 6 (Nov. 1967), pp. 82-4.*

Hill. Not even tourists can reach the Acropolis on Friday, the 21st. Later, jet fighters will buzz the city in fancy formations. And a whole squadron of warships is soon to anchor, intimidatingly, in Piraeus Bay.

You can buy English and Paris-published American papers the same day of their publication, usually toward the late afternoon [Fodor's *Greece, 1966*].

Like hell you can! The "latest" papers, dated 20 April, have already begun to yellow in clothes-pinned tiers at downtown kiosks. The headlines— in English, German, French, and Italian—proclaim Adenauer's death. Each day he seems to die afresh. The blackout is a really touching display of confidence in their own citizenry by the new government.... "Censorship of the press," claimed Col. Papadopoulos, the prime minister's aide, "even during the first five days had been interpreted so broadly that it had no connection at all with the censorship of other times." The colonel must be a careful student of Greek Mythology.... As just how great a pack of simpletons does the *Putsch* regime regard the public when it peddles as fact that "documentary evidence" for the planned Communist takeover filled no less than 70 3-ton trucks!... Two young German travelers aboard the Athens–Munich "Hellenic Express" think that a stern military government may be exactly what Greece needs for perhaps two years. To end party wrangling and restore order. Which is just how their parents probably reasoned some 34 years ago when the little Austrian Corporal promised to straighten things out.... What has proven more disturbing than the calamity suffered by Greece itself is the indifference—if not *sympathy*—demonstrated by foreigners here toward the coup. I have yet to meet *one* who feels a "gut reaction" to the sight of tanks and bayonets on city streets....

*Soviet Union, June 5-20.* To Russian readers, the "latest" and most popular American writers are Steinbeck, Frost, Hemingway, and Dreiser. Baldwin, Henry Miller, Mailer, Heller, Selby, Bellow, Patchen, Rexroth, Ellison, W.C. Williams, Ginsberg, LeRoi Jones, Corso, Burroughs, Ferlinghetti (who in January appeared with Andrei Voznesensky, the Soviet bard, at a dual poetry reading in West Berlin's Akademie Der Kunste): None of these names evoked even a glimmer of recognition ... and although a few Russians could identify Peter Weiss—alone among contemporary authors— it seems that none of his work has yet been published in the Soviet Union, nor has "Marat/Sade" appeared on any Russian stage. No doubt it's much too ambiguous. Not nearly positive nor inspiring enough (like the thousands of gleaming white, bigger-than-life, mass-produced figures—heroic workers, farmers, athletes, and cosmonauts—that grace the Soviet roadside)....

A bronze or stone Lenin, arm outstretched in exhortation, dominates the Main Square in nearly every village and town. His earnest visage inhabits countless posters. A whole museum in Moscow traces and exalts his life, while hordes of ordinary citizens every day wait patiently in line for hours to glimpse his embalmed cadaver outside the Kremlin walls. But nowhere could I find a single bust, portrait, or photo of Leon Trotsky. "Rootless cosmopolitan," "left deviationist," "counter-revolutionary traitor," he has slipped completely and silently down the Orwellian "memory hole". . . . The only foreign-language newspapers freely available at kiosks and libraries are CP organs like the French *L'Humanite,* British *Morning Star,* East German *Neues Deutschland,* and *American Worker.* . . . On the German-language shelves of the Kursk Public Library sits a DDR-produced critical study of postwar German poetry (Grass, Enzensberger, Celan, etc.), but the library stocks no *whole* book of verse by any of the "interpreted" writers; readers must be satisfied with a few tantalizing excerpts supplied by the East German critic to suit his own ends. . . . At Chernotsky, over jiggers of vodka, two well-groomed, smooth-talking chaps insisted that Sinyavsky and Daniel fully deserved long prison sentences for publishing "seditious propaganda" abroad (e.g., *The Trial Begins,* a novel written under the joint pseudonym "Abram Tertz"). Naturally, their whole knowledge of the case derived solely from Soviet press reports. They had never read the condemned articles and books, only the meager, out-of-context quotations made by the prosecutor in court. . . . Just days before the Middle East crisis erupted into war, vituperation against Israel overflowed the Soviet airways and editorial columns. Yet a schoolteacher in Or'ol admitted — although reluctantly — he had *never* read nor heard that Arab leaders for years have stridently, openly vowed to exterminate the Jewish state. . . . Jews, incidentally, account for 40% of the Chernotsky population, but no public school offers instruction in either Hebrew or Yiddish. Similarly, 300,000 Jews live in Moscow, where there is not even *one* kosher restaurant. . . . To say "Marc Chagall" is to invite blank stares. "Igor Stravinsky" wins much the same reaction. (The solitary Stravinsky score I noticed for sale in a Moscow music shop was "Petrouschka." Nice, but hardly his most recent or pioneering work.) . . . At the Bolshoi, a brilliantly-danced ballet, "Assel," *premiered* only a month earlier. Yet Tschaikovsky might have composed the music. . . . And from the pretty lips of a guide at the Turgenev Museum: "Russia can do without any of *us,* but we cannot do without Russia. . . ." Now, on a brighter note: a Moscow University student, after bitterly relating how authorities had suddenly banned — one day after it opened — an exhibit of modern art by young Russian painters and sculptors, resolutely declared, "We are not as stupid as our government thinks. . . ." He warmly endorsed the letter by Alexander Solzhenitsyn (author of *One Day in the Life of Ivan Denisovich*), still circulating privately among Russian intellectuals, which sharply citicizes literary censorship. "Literature," Solzhenitsyn maintains, "cannot develop between the categories 'Permitted' and 'Not Permitted.' Literature which does not breathe the same air as contemporary society, which cannot communicate to society its pains and fears, which cannot give warning in time against moral and social dangers, does not deserve the name of literature. . . ." And the Student Drama Club at Kiev's Foreign-Language Institute is currently producing "Who's Afraid of Virginia Woolf?"

A few news items and reports from West Germany, published in *Vorgange*
and *Mitteilungen,* both issued by the Humanistische Union (roughly
equivalent to the ACLU):

The movie industry's Self-Regulating Board [Filmselbst Kontrolle] in
Wiesbaden lately refused permission for "Changers in the Temple" [Die
Wechsler in Tempel], a short film, to be screened publicly. According to the
board, the film tendentiously falsifies historical truth and offends religious
sensibilities. A first Examining Committee earlier reached this same verdict
with a smaller majority; the second (so-called Main Committee) actually approved the film; while the third (Legal Committee) finally declared the ban
after a 5-hour long debate.... Since then, local HU and HSU [Human-
istische Studentenunion] groups have privately shown the movie, afterwards conducting open discussions on the issues it raises, especially whether
any body or organization can properly determine for the whole populace
what is "Christian" or "Unchristian."—*Mitteilungen,* 26/1966.

In September 1958, 54% of the [West German] respondents in a nationwide opinion poll believed that the public should be forbidden to read books
or view films authorized censors find "improper."

A comparative international study revealed Germany in eighth place
among populations favoring censorship (behind Venezuela, Belgium,
Brazil, Columbia, Austria, Japan, and Mexico), while Australia (48% for,
48% against), Norway (45% to 40%), Argentina (45% to 52%), and
England (41% to 56%) followed. However, the Federal Republic (41%)
leads all other countries in the conviction that "the government" should be
responsible for censorship, preceding Austria and Brazil (each 39%),
Australia and Norway (both 14%), as well as England (11%).—Heinz E.
Wolf, "Vorurteile und Toleranz in Der Bundesrepublik" ["Prejudice and
Tolerance in the Federal Republic"] *Vorgange,* Mai 1967.

The HU has undertaken legal action against the Federal Film Import
Board, which recently prohibited a Munich organization, the "Filmforum
Jugend-film-werk," from releasing an East German-produced documentary
on the notorious mercenary-major, "Kongo-Muller" (a former *Wehrmacht*
officer hired by Joseph Mobutu to crush Congolese "rebels"). In its brief, the
HU sharply criticized the Board's practice of precensorship and further
noted that although the governing statute provided for supervision [Uber-
wachung] of *all* foreign films, some 140 countries have since been exempted,
leaving only movies from East-Bloc lands still subject to control. "If the object," concluded the HU, "is really to safeguard democracy and promote
mutual understanding among peoples ... then motion pictures imported
from these other 140 states must also be placed under Federal scrutiny. At
present, for example, "Kongo-Muller," a DDR-production, may be pro-
scribed, but a blatantly racist film from Italy ["Africa Addio"] undergoes no
review whatever... —summarized from *Mitteilungen,* 30/Feb.–Mar.–Apr.
1967.

I might add that just a week ago I saw "Kongo-Muller" myself, at a special showing in Stuttgart's TH (Technical University). The local SDS (German Socialist Student Organization) had somehow secured a non-commercial copy. It was most instructive.

# LETTER FROM STUTTGART

Commercial pilots are subject to political danger at Arab airports. In a circular letter, German Lufthansa warns its flight-captains that customs officials in Tripolis (Libya) and Tunis (Tunisia) confiscate all magazines and newspapers aboard landed aircraft. If pictures or reports in the seized publications are declared "anti-Arabic," the flight-captains are held responsible and may face imprisonment. — *Der Spiegel,* 24 July 1967, p. 20.

Also, on 20 July Munich authorities destroyed some 100,000 copies — practically the whole run — of issue no. 29 of the *National und Soldaten-Zeitung,* a right-wing, pro–NPD weekly. Its first page had juxtaposed photos of Hitler and Moshe Dayan. A seldom-invoked West German statute prohibits the reproduction of Nazi symbols. The NSZ is a most unpleasant paper and the Dayan-Hitler comparison was surely tasteless. Still, the government acted under a palpably flimsy pretext, for swastikas and Hitler-pictures often appear in West German publications (for example, on the 24 July *Spiegel* cover, as well as p. 93). Tastelessness, strident nationalism, and flagrant bias are to be expected from the NSZ. They come as no surprise. But it *is* distressing that the West German press seems whole-heartedly to have approved what can only be described as an instance of crass political censorship. It is a hard lesson to learn: that freedom is even for people we don't like.

*Reprinted with permission from* Newsletter on Intellectual Freedom, *v. 16, no. 6 (Nov. 1967), p. 76.*

# PREXY SONG

I'm for Locke and I'm for Milton.
I'm for speaking without fear.
I'm for Academic Freedom
Almost anyplace but here.

*Reprinted with permission from* Newsletter on Intellectual Freedom, *v. 16, no. 3 (May 1967), p. 26.*

# SOUTH AFRICAN
# CENSORSHIP

November 3, 1971

Dear Editors:

Frankly, I'm furious. I've read much and myself written a little on South African censorship, but not until this morning was I *personally* confronted with its concrete reality. To be specific: Some months ago I ordered for the Makerere Institute of Social Research Library a copy of *Some Implications of Inequality,* Spro-Cas Occasional publication no. 4, a 1971, booklet-sized collection of four papers published by the Study Project on Christianity in Apartheid Society (P.O. Box 31134, Johannesburg). This week it arrived, and only moments ago I opened the volume to begin cataloging. This is how the contents' page looks:

## CONTENTS

| | |
|---|---:|
| What is Spro-Cas? | 9 |
| Introduction | 11 |
| Notes on the papers | 12 |
| Distress in the Reserves: | 13 |
| e. a. barker | |
| Malnutrition: | 17 |
| j.v.o. reid | |
| Poverty: | 40 |
| h. l. watts | |
| ~~African resettlement:~~ | 58 |
| ~~c. desmond~~ | |

And, affixed to the top, a slender insertion-slip:

*Reprinted with permission from* Newsletter on Intellectual Freedom, *v. 21, no. 1 (January 1972), pp. 2, 9.*

PUBLISHERS' NOTE:

In view of the fact that a banning order has been served on the Rev. C. Desmond, the final paper in this publication has had to be taken out.

Page 57 I found neatly snipped below the last (12th) footnote of Watts' piece on "Poverty," and overleaf only Desmond's title,

~~AFRICAN RESETTLEMENT,~~

lined-out. After that, nothing. Merely three blank leaves.

"Father [Cosmas] Desmond," according to 'Notes on the papers' (p. 12), "is a Franciscan priest whose concern about the resettlement of Africans in South Africa resulted in the publication by the Christian Institute of his book, *The Discarded People,* in 1970." (Excerpts from that work, incidentally, appeared in the August 1971 *Sechaba,* pp. 14–17.)

Well, like I said, I'm angry. But at least the opportunity to report this piece of otherwise-incredible totalitarian madness slightly relieves that anger.

Yours,

Signed: Sanford Berman
Librarian

P.S. Should I tonight find in my own back-copies of *Spotlight on South Africa,* an ANC-produced news digest, more data on Fr. Desmond's "banning," I'll forward them tomorrow.

November 4, 1971

Dear Editors:

As a postscript to yesterday's letter. . .

The London *Times* on 29 June 1971 carried the following report, later reprinted in *Spotlight on South Africa: News Digest,* v. 9, no. 24 (2 July 1971), p. 2:

The South African Government has placed Father Cosmas Desmond, a British-born Roman Catholic priest, under arrest at his home in Johannesburg. Father Desmond, author of *The Discarded People,* a study of conditions in African resettlement areas, was also concerned in making the British television film, *The Dumping Ground,* which dealt with African resettlement in the republic. Orders, signed by Petrus Pelser, the Minister of Justice, and handed to Father Desmond today, confine him to his home from 6 p.m. to 7 a.m. on weekdays and all day on Saturdays and Sundays. He is banned from attending gatherings, confined to the Johannesburg district, and may not enter any African, Coloured or Asian area. . . . A member of the Franciscan order, Father Desmond, aged 35, is a research worker for the Christian Institute. The house arrest order will deprive him of his livelihood, according to friends. He has been living on the proceeds of his book and on freelance journalism. As he is now banned, he may no longer be quoted in South Africa nor may his writings be published here. Father Desmond came to South Africa from Britain in 1959, and became a South African citizen in 1968.

A subsequent news-item, quoted on p. 3 of the 9 July *Spotlight* from the 2 July *Rand Daily Mail,* disclosed that

The Minister of Justice, Mr. Pelser, yesterday refused a request for a relaxation of Father Cosmas Desmond's house arrest order to allow the Franciscan priest to attend Sunday mass.

In sum, the fantastic absence of intellectual freedom south of the Limpopo, the all-pervasive, mind-stifling, state-executed censorship described in detail by authorities like Ezekiel Mphahlele (e.g., "Censorship in South Africa," *Censorship Today,* v. 2, no. 4, Aug.–Sept. 1969), is real enough. For visual proof, one need only have a look at the nearest mutilated copy of Spro-Cas occasional publication no. 4. And, of course, the widely-hailed *Discarded People* has now become, at least in the Republic, a *non*-book.

Yours,

Signed: Sanford Berman
Librarian
Makerere Institute of
Social Research
Kampala, Uganda

# IFLA AND RACISM

The New York *Times* on 23 January 1972 reported that UNESCO "has broken off contacts" with some 42 international organizations "that have branches, affiliates or operations in South Africa, Rhodesia, and the Portuguese colonies in Africa." Thomas J. Hamilton, the *Times'* Geneva-based correspondent, elaborated that UNESCO's Executive Board in Paris "suspended 'consultative status' with the organizations because they had neither expelled branches nor submitted proof that branches do not practice racial discrimination or support racial policies." About midway down the published list of suspended groups appears the International Federation of Library Associations (IFLA), with which many national library associations are affiliated. [The 1970/71 *World of learning* on p. 28 reveals that IFLA is composed of "81 associations, representing 47 countries and 5 international associations," together with "150 associate members."] Noting this, several American librarians intend to put the following resolution before the Executive Board of the American Library Association, due to meet in late April this year:

> Whereas the American Library Association is committed to human rights and social justice, regardless of origin, color, creed, race, country, or religion; and
>
> Whereas the American Library Association honors these commitments through the activities of its members organizationally and individually; and
>
> Whereas the American Library Association is a member of the International Federation of Library Associations (IFLA), which has lost its consultative status with UNESCO on grounds of racial discrimination; be it therefore
>
> Resolved, that the American Library Association immediately terminate its membership in, and all relationships with, IFLA, until its consultative status is restored by UNESCO; and be it further
>
> Resolved, that the American Library Association shall have no affiliations with or memberships in other organizations which violate its principles and commitments to human rights and social justice.

*Reprinted from* MISR Library Accessions List/Bulletin, *March 1972, p. 25.*

If librarians the world over are, indeed, committed to "human rights and social justice," there should soon be a general blossoming of similar resolutions. Not only does the proposed ALA resolution merit support from American colleagues, but Africans themselves might well "start the ball rolling" by threatening IFLA with disaffiliation unless it promptly submits to UNESCO the requisite "proof that branches do not practice racial discrimination or support racial policies." The OAU and most African governments have justly thundered against both Apartheid and continuing colonialism on the continent. Now librarians have a ready-made opportunity to echo those sentiments with concrete acts. Will they?

# PALATNIK/TRACHTENBERG CASE

The October 1971 *Assistant librarian* (volume 64, number 10) devoted four pages to "The agony of Reizia Palatnik," a Soviet librarian relentlessly humiliated and ultimately jailed simply because "she was born a Jew." The December 1971 *AL* (volume 64, number 12) reported still another instance of anti-Semitic persecution: the imprisonment of Amaliat Trachtenberg, aged 45, who "received a three year ... sentence after she wrote to Soviet leaders complaining about discrimination against the Jews and asking to be allowed to emigrate." According to *AL* (December 1971, page 188), the Association of Assistant Librarians' Council has approved a motion requesting that the parent Library Association "condemn publicly the actions of the Russian Government and the KGB" in Palatnik's case. Other library associations may wish to follow suit, perhaps also incorporating Trachtenberg in their declarations. Fellow professionals who find these acts equally as reprehensible as the sort of racism lately denounced by UNESCO, which led to the suspension of "consultative status" for a number of NGOs (including the IFLA), might propose to their respective groups a resolution like the following, to be disseminated — if passed — not only to the usual news media, but also to the Soviet Government and Russian library profession:

THE ... LIBRARY ASSOCIATION vigorously condemns the deliberate harassment of Reizia Palatnik and Amaliat Trachtenberg, both Russian librarians and Jews, by the Soviet Government and KGB, as reported in the October and December 1971 issues of the *Assistant librarian*.

FURTHER, THE ASSOCIATION demands that these two colleagues, unjustly imprisoned because of their faith and ethnic background, be immediately released and either promptly reinstated in their former positions, or, if they so choose, permitted to emigrate.

Those among us who feel that the plight of Palatnik and Trachtenberg is unfortunate but hardly germane to librarians elsewhere might well ponder *AL*'s comment on that point (October 1971, page 145): "To say that we — the

*Reprinted from* MISR Library Accessions List/Bulletin, *April 1972, p. 30.*

library profession — must not involve ourselves in such political issues is to dodge the issue. Such an attitude can be of little comfort to a girl lying seriously ill in an Odessa prison." No arbitrary boundaries of nationality, race, or religion can circumscribe the realm of books and libraries. It is global. Thus Palatnik and Trachtenberg, just as all the oppressed, "second-class" Black librarians in Southern Africa, are *our* co-workers.

# UGANDA: SPEAK IN WHISPERS, IF AT ALL

In late September, 1972, my family and I returned to the States from Uganda. For 18 months I'd worked at the Makerere Institute of Social Research (MISR), which occupies a verdant corner of the vast university campus in Kampala, the capital, an attractive, many-hilled city only a few miles from Lake Victoria's shimmering waters. We left that idyllic scene joylessly and rather abruptly, due to a worsening political situation that not only rendered daily work difficult but also endangered us personally. In fact, I had already suspended publication of the MISR Library's monthly *Accessions list/bulletin,* despite acclaim from its worldwide readership, largely because I no longer felt able to editorialize freely on problems of intellectual freedom and racism in Uganda itself. (Earlier issues had variously castigated H.W. Wilson's *Library literature* for inadequate Black African coverage, proposed international action by librarians to win release of imprisoned Russian-Jewish colleagues, exposed new eruptions of South African censorship, and assaulted racist and chauvinist bias in Western subject schema.) Too many outspoken critics, as well as "suspected" opponents, of the Amin Regime, installed by a coup on January 25, 1971, either "disappeared," suffered periodic beatings, lost their jobs, were summarily deported (if "expatriates"), or were intimidated by public threats and rebukes.

The repression-roster included the Chief Justice, a Governor of the Bank of Uganda, the Catholic Archbishop, and a *People* editor, all Black. According to press reports, many members of certain "undesirable" ethnic groups, especially Lango and Acholi, had been bludgeoned to death. "Loyalist" troops, including numerous Congolese and Sudanese mercenaries, bloodily "purged" these same groups from the Army a year before. Army "brass" enjoy full authority to arrest whomever they wish. Habeas Corpus? An irrelevant, moribund concept. Political parties? None. Abolished. They only foment "confusion." (So does a strong labor movement.)

*Reprinted with permission from* Newsletter on Intellectual Freedom, *March 1973, pp. 27, 40-1.*

Last summer, the very regime that so stridently trumpets about "African unity" banished all Senegalese from the country and further intimated that thousands of Rwandan refugees may shortly be "repatriated" to a homeland unlikely to welcome them back with much enthusiasm. The Chief of State repeatedly vilified Presidents Nyerere and Kaunda for rightly and bravely condemning his "Asian Policy" as both racist and inhumane. He ludicrously accused the Tanzanian leader, in particular, of undermining African liberation movements. He hautily rebuffed President Mobutu of neighboring Zaire, who sought to soften the harsher aspects of Amin's Asian-program. And Amin ceremoniously awarded Uganda's highest decoration to the Central African Republic's General Bokassa, who some years ago distinguished himself by fighting *with* the French Army *against* Ho Chi Minh.

Radio and television became handy vehicles for "scare" diversions. On one day they warned of an approaching British armada. On the next, of Indian warships steaming toward East Africa. And on the third, of a joint Israeli-Rwandan "imperialist" plot to overthrow the Second Republic. At one point, the General broadcast that the 7,000 Britons in Uganda, potential "subversives," must be closely watched by police and army. On another occasion, he invited the populace to see the semi-mutilated body of a captured "Red Chinese guerrilla," who — it transpired — fit none of those categories. An unending torrent of scapegoats and frightful fantasies. Indeed, this pattern of unrelenting terror, calumny, scapegoating, and Big Lies has since intensified, paralyzing much of Ugandan society.

The future of Makerere University, long the cornerstone of higher education in East Africa, now seems uncertain. The black Vice-Chancellor, a reputable senior civil servant, "vanished" last month. Paratroopers swarmed over the campus on October 12, only abandoning their "patrols" more than a week later. At least seventy expatriate staff, among them several librarians and all but one lecturer at the East African School of Librarianship, have resigned or fled within the past three months. The National Union of Students has been banned, the most prominent student leaders "detained," the student body personally warned by the President "not to talk about politics if you don't want to get into trouble." Two British medical school professors were deported for promoting "political gonorrhea" (i.e., voicing concern at the Asians' plight and purportedly advising other foreigners to leave). The budget was slashed by 20 percent. Campus sources relate that a third of M.U.K.'s students failed to appear for the start of the current term, and it's rumored that the Economics Department has wholly shut down. If true, this could represent the beginning of a cycle leading to complete closure as students, staff, and funds alike rapidly diminish.

Even before I left, normal library work, research, and teaching had become nearly hopeless. People tended to speak in whispers, if at all, and carefully wrote nothing of consequence for publication or in private letters. ("How are you? We are fine. It's a beautifully sunny day here. Multicolored birds, in a wondrous variety of sizes and shapes noisily twitter, whistle, or squawk outside. Bamboo turns radiantly golden at sunset. Dined tonight on Nile Perch. Delicious, as always. Love.") All registered mail and parcels, the Government announced, would be thoroughly examined. Most ordinary letters now bear the censor's stamp.

Nearly every embassy soberly cautioned its nationals against travel outside the capital. One Peace Corpsman had been shot fatally and another manhandled while returning from a game park. Tourists had been roughly searched, and passengers aboard Kenya-bound trains often told of mistreatment, even robbery, by soldiers. Some embassies arranged for particularly vulnerable or "sensitive" persons, such as women, children, Jews, interracial families, and remotely-stationed volunteer workers, to leave. The Government had for many months waged a non-stop, anti–Semitic propaganda campaign, indiscriminately branding all Jews as "Zionist conspirators" or "Israeli CIA agents." Troops frequently hassled racially-mixed couples, usually assuming the woman to be Ugandan, in the clumsy belief that such liaisons amounted to "treason." In the meantime, the Government itself, headed by a Muslim who regularly claims intimate communication with Allah, has expelled scores of Christian missionaries. Practically the entire foreign press corps previously underwent the same fate, many first being jailed at Makindye Prison, during the abortive September invasion. As a result, reasonably accurate reportage on current Ugandan events is at a premium, for no local media dare to contradict or criticize the official version of what's happening.

During the summer, the military *jefes*—extremely puritanical and sexist in temper—banned mini-skirts, "hot pants," and "slits," an act that provoked serious mob-attacks upon many young women and compelled much of the female population to spend hard-to-come-by shillings on more dress-material (most of it imported). Beards, being equated with decadent "hippies," were nearly prohibited. Many men—black, white, and brown—nevertheless shaved. Just in case. Longhair visitors are *non grata,* either thought to be spies or "bad influences." Movies close early in the evening, bars at one a.m. And the khaki moralists arbitrarily tabooed teenage dances.

Our chief anxiety after leaving centered on the roughly 10,000 Asians, who, once the November 8th expulsion deadline arrived, faced internment in concentration camps and, should President Amin's explicit endorsement of Hitler's "Final Solution" become transmuted into Government policy, possible annihilation. Reports alleged that impatient soldiers had already kidnapped or brutalized countless Asians in "up-country" areas. Subsequently, the Government decreed that all remaining Asians, mainly *citizens,* must vacate the large towns and settle in the countryside, ostensibly to get better "assimilated." The actual effect of that edict is likely to be not "assimilation," but rather extermination, for the forcibly-resettled Asians are primarily shopkeepers and *fundis* (artisans) who will either find it impossible to sustain themselves in small villages or will be subject to the not-so-tender mercy of Uganda's notoriously uncontrollable, racism-infected "security forces." Beyond that, even if this resettlement "worked," it would constitute — as Amerindians, Chicanos, Puerto Ricans, and Afro-Americans will readily appreciate — a clearcut case of ethnocide.

Anyone automatically inclined to sympathize with General Amin's rhetoric about "economic independence," "Africanization," and the need to eliminate Asian "bloodsuckers" might well consider that the highly-touted "Economic War" derived from a sudden, overnight, "divine" revelation, which hardly permitted any substantial advance planning to suitably replace the soon-to-be-expelled Asian entrepreneurs, clerks, administrators, builders, professionals, and manufacturers. The impact on Uganda's economy of this instant, massive loss of trained manpower will be disastrous unless comparably skilled persons can be recruited to fill the vacuum. But the immediate prospects for that are dim. Additionally, the expulsion was unarguably *racist* in that it made little or no distinction between citizens and non-citizens, individuals engaged in mercantile and strictly service or professional activities, the young and the aged. Examining officials commonly destroyed bona fide citizenship documents and birth certificates, thus deliberately reducing hundreds of citizen-Asians to statelessness. Fortunately, many of these people, together with thousands of those holding foreign passports, managed — partly through the U.N. High Commission for Refugees and the Red Cross — to reach sanctuary in Malta, Malawi, Austria, Italy, Canada, Britain, and elsewhere. America reluctantly accepted 1,000. The "crusade" equally affected *all* Asians — solely on the basis of being *Asian,* determined simply by their appearance and Indic names — regardless of whether they had been born in the country, regarded it as their genuine, permanent home, or performed undeniably valuable functions as doctors, teachers, librarians, nurses, magistrates, civil servants, etc. Since last year's special "census," offensively conducted on the day of the Hindu Diwali celebration, the Asian community, *en masse,* has been incessantly defamed and maligned in such racist, inflammatory terms as "saboteurs," "exploiters," and "so-called yellowish citizens." This dehumanization barrage (similar to our own "Yellow Peril" hysteria and South Africa's Apartheid/White Supremacist vocabulary) stemmed directly from the Government, in tandem with local mass-media. One Kampala paper, for example, boldly declared: "We hate the Asians. They should have been driven out long ago at gunpoint." (Parenthetically, Leicester, a British city, in half-page newspaper ads callously informed would-be Asian immigrants that they weren't wanted there.) An almost irresistible explanation — given the facts that *some* Asians essentially monopolized the distributive sector and the majority, since they composed much of the "middle class," had money in the bank plus cars, houses, and real estate — is that the Government hoped to achieve a two-fold objective: to lessen growing Treasury and foreign-exchange deficits (products of lavish military expenditures) by ultimately expropriating Asian assets and property, as well as permitting Army officers and other favored elite–Ugandans to aggrandize themselves by taking over Asian enterprises and goods. The Government allowed Asians to depart with a mere $150 in cash and minimal personal belongings. Left-behind shops and factories were registered for later "re-sale" to Africans and bank-balances were "frozen." That any of these people, now scattered across the globe, many of whom had literally invested their lives in the country, will ever receive even a nominal "compensation" seems doubtful.

Apart from the pandering to their historic anti–Asian prejudice, ordinary black Ugandans will probably not reap much benefit from the dozens of closed shops, increasing shortages, severely limited or eroded services, and rampant, ever-stronger "barrel of the gun" tyranny. The "Asian Question," in reality, was a decoy, a mystification, to begin with, inasmuch as *external* interests really dominate the economy, and Asians — obviously — wielded little or no *political* power. The imports retailed by Asian *dukawallahs* emanated from Europe and Japan. Overseas, predominantly British conglomerates granted auto-distribution and like franchises. Asians might manage a tea plantation or gas station, but the likelihood — verifiable in *Who Owns Whom* — is that European corporations owned them.

As I've stated in a brief letter to *American Libraries*, persons planning to work or travel in Uganda should be dissuaded from doing so. At this moment, certainly, it is not a safe place to be. And colleagues of whatever ethnic background who value professional integrity, personal freedom, and fundamental human rights, will find the present atmosphere — rule by a "lumpen militariat" — insufferable. Yes, the Amin regime is "Black." Yet, nonetheless, a menace to Pan-Africanism, to Third World solidarity, and — sadly, if also ironically — to Uganda itself.

# "THE SPEAKER":
# NOT RECOMMENDED

A high school student current events committee decides—for wholly unclear reasons—to invite a Dr. Boyd, who espouses Black inferiority, to speak at the school's Spring Assembly. Following that decision, students, teachers, administrators, and the outside community urge the committee to retract its invitation. The committee, however, supported by its about-to-retire faculty advisor, refuses. Ultimately, the school administration cancels the Doctor's appearance. And viewers are explicitly informed, in this 42-minute "film about freedom," that the First Amendment has been severely, though not irreparably, damaged.

The movie is erroneously subtitled. It is less a "film about freedom" than a "film about foolishness" or—more gravely—about "bigotry and defamation." The "freedom" issue is a phoney, the plot entirely contrived, the dialogue cliche-ridden, the characters stereotypic and classist (e.g., the two opera-lovers are both pro-speaker), and the overall cinematic execution, simply dull.

A few specifics:

The film promotes a vision of serious unreality concerning intellectual freedom problems in schools and libraries. In fact, such incidents—i.e., disputes over a Burt/Jensen/Shockley-like speaker—are uncommon in either high schools or libraries. As the literature (including OIF's own newsletter) amply documents, the overwhelmingly typical cases of censorship and suppression involve sex, politics, and religion—the "baddies" or First Amendment wasters being not Blacks nor liberals, but rather conservatives and fundamentalists, usually White. (My personal experience in military, college, and public libraries also confirms this.)

The film wrongly implies that the current events committee somehow was *obligated* to invite Dr. Boyd because he enjoys a right to "freedom of expression." In actuality, the First Amendment *permits* Dr. Boyd to think, say

*Reprinted with permission from* Interracial Books for Children Bulletin, *v.8, nos. 4/5 (1977), pp. 19-20.*

or write whatever he wishes — *but* it imposes no requirement on any citizen or group (the current events committee included) to *consume* Dr. Boyd's products. Nor is it, as the movie alleges, "repression" to boycott or ignore Dr. Boyd. *He* has no absolute First Amendment right to speak at a given place or time — like the high school's Spring Assembly — *without* being invited. In short, not inviting him is not equivalent to *repressing* him or his opinions. Indeed, the film irresponsibly distorts what "repression" really is: e.g., government-conducted murder and sabotage against the Black Panthers, the confinement of Soviet dissidents in psychiatric hospitals and labor camps, the numberless "disappearances" in Uganda, the spiralling "suicides" among apartheid critics in South African jails, torture in Uruguay, bookburnings in Chile, etc.

The film mistakenly equates inviting someone to speak on a particular topic (like the genetic inferiority of Blacks or women) with stocking various library materials on that same topic. The speaking engagement is just not comparable, for it takes place at a unique moment in time, in this case would have afforded a podium to only *one* side of a topic, enjoys special publicity and commands a sizeable, guaranteed audience. Library materials, by contrast, ideally express or reflect a multitude of "sides" or opinions on a given subject, and are all simultaneously accessible. They are not time-bound nor is any *one* aspect of a controversy automatically and unfairly highlighted. (An obvious compromise solution to the filmatic "conflict" would have been to transform the solo event into a debate, but this never even emerged as an option.)

The film fails to confront what is utterly crucial to the whole issue: the Black clergyman's point that to gratuitously raise the "question" or possibility of racial inferiority is in effect to legitimize the "theory" or "attitude" itself. That is, given the potential variety and extent of speakers and topics from which to choose, *why* should the committee select someone who propagates *racial inferiority,* a belief or contention that a) is not an important scientific nor contemporary controversy; b) by its very nature is anti–Constitutional (i.e., denying the Constitution's — and our society's — necessary and basic assumption of human equality irrespective of purely physical/biological differences); and c) does not, except by means of incredibly warped logic, qualify as one of those grand, historic, initially "unpopular" and scorned ideas that later came into general acceptance and enriched our civilization! (The "idea" here is not that the earth is round or rotates around the sun. It is racism: that Black people are genetically deficient. And racism, in any event, has hardly been an "unpopular" notion. Far from it.) It would have proven much more interesting and instructive to examine why the Committee made the choice it did, to contest its judgment, and to suggest that mature reconsideration of its decision could lead to an honest admission of error — without introducing the "censorship" or "free speech" bugaboo.

Ironically, the very instance cited of U.S. governmental repression — the Japanese internment during World War II — did not stem from gradually eroded "freedoms" (as the film pointedly claims), but rather from longstanding racism, precisely the kind of "theory" promulgated/reinforced/legitimized by Boyd/Burt/Jensen/Shockley. The film so facilely and single-mindedly states its thesis about the danger of free-speech constraints that it grotesquely ignores the colossal, abundantly-demonstrated danger of racism. Actually, the two problems need not collide. By counterposing them, the film does not destroy the opponents of intellectual freedom (who in the real world are most unlike the Black/liberal stick-figures portrayed on the screen). Instead, it destroys itself.

I had not thought it possible that a professional library association could produce a film about intellectual freedom that made the very concept seem dirty. Now I know better.

Not recommended.

# *JAKE*—AND LIBRARY
# ISSUES OF SELECTION

*Jake and Honeybunch* has been the center of much controversy lately because public library systems in Chicago, Milwaukee and San Francisco, finding the work racist and stereotypic, decided either to limit purchase or not buy it at all. These decisions sparked the classic responses to charges of racism. The publisher—Farrar, Straus & Giroux—labelled the claims "bizarre," counter-charging that the libraries committed censorship by not purchasing the book. Or not purchasing it in suitable quantities. (Presumably, any public library not selecting at least one copy—and any large system not buying multiples—of *each* of the 40,000 English-language trade titles published yearly in the U.S. has "censored" the un- or under-bought books!) Farrar, after enunciating that quaint theory of book selection, released its correspondence with the objecting librarians to *The New York Times,* which caused some to wonder if publicity (rather than indignation over "censorship") wasn't the real "name of the game." (The *Times* report did, however, provide some merriment. When Farrar's editor-in-chief of children's books asked San Francisco why it decided not to buy *Jake,* City Librarian John C. Frantz replied, "If he really doesn't know . . . he is in the wrong line of work and should be selling banjos to minstrel troupes.")

Elsewhere—for instance, at a Minneapolis censorship conference in January—ALA's Judy Krug similarly denounced her erstwhile Chicago and San Francisco colleagues for *not* selecting *Jake.* And for saying *why* they rejected it. Krug had bought a copy for herself, liked the pretty pictures, couldn't imagine how anyone would judge it "racist," and in any event doesn't regard "racism" as a valid selection factor. (Parenthetically, she directed far more fury at those benighted children's librarians than at the KKK, which in Indiana had just joined the campaign to remove pro-gay material from a public library. She was also enraged that the Farrar-librarian exchange *appeared in the press.* And this, remember, is the Director of ALA's *Intellectual Freedom* Office!)

*Reprinted with permission from* Interracial Books for Children Bulletin, *v. 14, no. 5 (1983), p. 3.*

Well, what does it all mean? In a way, Krug's right, for the official ALA statement "regulating" book selection, *Diversity in Collection Development,* which supplanted its earlier *Racism, Sexism, and Other -Isms in Library Materials* policy, does appear to exclude considerations of "cultural authenticity" and "defamatory stereotyping" from the selection process. In other words, it seems to declare that being inauthentic or stereotypic is not sufficient reason to weed or reject a work.

If nothing else, the *Jake* furor **should** pinpoint two key issues:

**1.** Whether authenticity and stereotyping should be selection criteria.

**2.** Whether children's materials should be selected according to somewhat different standards than adult.

While ALA's "Diversity" and "Free Access to Minors" statements ostensibly resolved these issues, in fact they have not.

At the premier, Los Angeles meeting of the Ethnic Materials Information Exchange (EMIE) Round Table in June, I personally proposed amendment of the "Diversity" statement during a small group discussion. Opinion within that group proved largely favorable, particularly since one speaker after another—including Spencer Shaw, Lotsee Smith and Suzine Har Nicolescu—had previously blasted the wretched quality of available material dealing with Blacks, Native Americans, Asian Americans and other groups. I want to repeat my proposal here, recommending amendment of the "Diversity" policy and/or adoption of a statement—perhaps via the EMIE Round Table, various caucuses, and the American Association of School Librarians—that specifically addresses juvenile materials selection and PERMITS considerations of cultural authenticity and derogatory stereotyping as bona fide selection criteria. For starters, here's a draft addition to the "Diversity" document that might be inserted immediately following "This includes materials that reflect political, economic, religious, social, minority and sexual issues":

> . . . , but does not preclude the non-selection of children's materials that are culturally inauthentic or that contain inaccurate, defamatory stereotypes of whole ethnic, racial, sexual, or other groups.

It's about time to make it an explicit, professional policy that works which misrepresent cultures or stereotype entire human groups have no more place in a children's collection than inaccurate chemistry and physics texts.

# ON BEYOND *JAKE:*
# A CALL TO DIALOG

For too many years children's rights advocates, First Amendment "purists," and social justice activists have battled within the American Library Association and elsewhere over the issue pinpointed in my previous editorial: whether children should be "protected" by library book and media selection policies that would keep inauthentic and stereotypic material out of juvenile circulating collections. Proponents say "Yes," arguing that pre-teen kids are not, in fact, "little adults" capable of critically evaluating racist, sexist, ageist or handicapist material, and that such items may do serious damage to children's self-identity, perhaps warping them for life. Opponents, on the other hand, maintain that children should enjoy the same, full access to library collections as adults and that invoking racism, sexism, ageism, or handicapism as selection criteria is tantamount to committing censorship. Often, the dispute becomes a contest between the First and Fourteenth Amendments: Free Speech vs. Equal Protection. And often it degenerates into name-calling and diatribe.

Believing that the issues are truly significant and that erstwhile combatants may — with good will — find some mutually common ground that does no violence to either First or Fourteenth Amendment rights, it seems appropriate to now issue a call for renewed dialog, which may freely take place in the *Bulletin*. And as a prelude to such dialog, here are several "propositions" to explore:

- There is an essential difference between material that attacks political, economic and religious ideas or groups and material that attacks people on the basis of unchangeable, physical, nonideological characteristics: age, gender, disability and ethnic/racial background.
- Children are more susceptible than teenagers or adults to identity-damaging stereotypes and group-defamation.
- Given the foregoing, library selection policies should explicitly deal

*Reprinted with permission from* Interracial Books for Children Bulletin, *v. 14, no. 6 (1983), p. 3.*

with the purpose, placement and supervised use of juvenile material that assaults or demeans persons or groups because of their immutable, involuntary characteristics.

Of course, none of this is quite as simple as it sounds. Proponents must demonstrate that stereotypic and defamatory material actually injures children. And they must establish at what age that sort of injury finally lessens. Similarly, intellectual freedom advocates need to consider if, indeed, a juvenile work that distorts the experience of a given ethnic or racial group, questions the humanity of young, older or disabled persons, or posits the superiority of men over women so violates Fourteenth Amendment strictures against denial of equal protection and due process that it just doesn't belong on the open shelves in a children's library collection. Further, they ought to seriously address the contention that one's changeable ideas or beliefs (*e.g.*, atheism, capitalism) are intrinsically unlike a person's immutable attributes (*e.g.*, race, sex).

We have been warring too long. And probably with the wrong adversaries. In a spirit of both intellectual freedom and child advocacy, let the dialog begin...

# THE LETTER THAT WASN'T

This missive, submitted to the editor of the *Jewish Librarians Caucus Newsletter* on December 8, 1982, has never been printed or even acknowledged, despite repeated queries:

Dear Colleague,

I co-founded the Jewish Librarians Caucus at the 1975 ALA Midwinter Meeting and have supported it ever since in the hope that JLC would aggressively fight anti-semitism inside librarianship and alert both Jewish and Gentile colleagues to resources and issues concerning Jewish Americans in all their diversity: religious and secular, gay and "straight," radical and traditional. What deeply troubles me is that the Caucus, in its acts and newsletter, seems increasingly to promote religious and Establishment interests, to ignore the growing progressive movement among American Jews (and Israelis, too!), and to abandon "the Jewish tradition . . . of equality and social justice for all people" (noted in the Caucus' original "Statement of Purpose") in favor of a reflexive, uncritical defense of Israeli government policy and corollary denigration of the Palestinian people.

In the October/December 1982 *Newsletter,* for instance:

*Inadequate media coverage of Afghan atrocities (page 5) becomes— through truly contorted logic—an argument for down-playing the Beirut Massacre. The implication: "Everybody massacres. It's no big thing. So why pick on Israelis?" In a larger context, what's remarkable is that the Beirut and Afghan events were reported at all. At approximately the same time, even *greater* massacres took place in Central America, but went virtually unnoticed in the press. The unfortunate truth is that atrocities and oppression suffered by Third World peoples seldom merit much attention. They are, after all, not White, not altogether "civilized" nor sweet-smelling. Not, in short, like us. A more appropriate JLC response to how the media treated Sabra-and-Shatila would have been to (a) applaud the in-depth reportage and rare "humanization" of Palestinians (usually, the implicit media formula is that one Israeli is worth at least two dozen Arabs); and (b) insist that *any*

*Reprinted from* Technicalities, *v. 4, no. 2 (Feb. 1984), pp. 6, 10, by permission of M.E. Sharpe, Inc., Armonk NY 10504.*

massacre, *any*where, demands the same sort of exposure and condemnation.

*A pro-Israeli brochure is described (page 5) as containing material on "the Palestinian Question." On the very next page appears another installment of my "'Jewish Question' in Library Cataloging." As is well known, I've denounced the term (and subject heading), "Jewish Question," as inherently biased and inaccurate, in effect rendering victims responsible for their own victimization. That's why I never record the phrase without quote-marks to suggest its dubious validity. No quote-marks, however, enclosed "Palestinian question," thus creating a noxious double-standard. Just as there never was a "Jewish *Question,*" only a problem of gaining fundamental rights for Jews wherever they lived and a secure homeland for those who wished or required it, so there is not now a "Palestinian *Question,*" only the problem of gaining fundamental rights for Palestinians wherever they live and a secure homeland for those who want or require it.

Under the caption, "West Bank University Planned for Jewish Settlers" (page 7), appears a news item on the development of a university in a "Jewish settlement on the West Bank" and the visit there of Edward Teller, "the American nuclear physicist." The tone, if anything, seems approving. But *what* is being approved? For one, further consolidation of alien rule (Israeli) over an indigenous population (Palestinians). For another, validation of the "Judea and Samaria" myth that for intelligent Jews should win about the same degree of acceptance as "scientific creationism." And finally, dear Dr. Teller's endorsement of anything ought to be viewed with some skepticism, since—unless I'm sorely mistaken—he is less a nuclear "physicist" than a nuclear hawk, a willing architect of what could easily prove a global holocaust and someone who has expressed no remorse over Hiroshima and Nagasaki. Talk about massacres....

SHALOM!

# ANOTHER LETTER
# THAT WASN'T

On August 14, 1984, I sent these remarks to *Small Press Review* (Dustbooks, P.O. Box 100, Paradise, CA 95969), which decided not to print them:

Dear Friends,

Three things about the August '84 *SPR:*

• The review of Alice Glarden Brand's *As It Happens* matter-of-factly acknowledges the poet's Jewishness and quotes explicitly "Jewish" passages from her work, like "something hides here/swastikas and Skokie, books about Eichmann/there's hardly a home without those books/and I wonder whose side they're on." As a preface to those lines, reviewer Shuey talks about "the insidious odor of anti-Semitism."

• Seven pages earlier, the "Guest Editorial" declares: "Present day majority readers have not only sent the Artists to the camps, they have systematically done to the people of culture what Hitler did to the Jews."

• On page 12 appears a sizeable ad for the latest *COSMEP Catalogue.*

Okay. Shuey's review coupled with Brand's verse-sampling impressed me enough to recommend that our Library order the book. But — ironically — that very "insidious odor of anti-Semitism" (or at least a stupendous insensitivity) emerges strongly from both the "Guest Editorial" and *COSMEP Catalogue* itself. While editorialists Berne and Zekowski may have intended their statement metaphorically, the historic and overpowering truth is that *no* comparison can be made between the plight of contemporary "Artists" and what European Jews suffered during the Holocaust. None. No artists have been consigned to concentration camps. No artists have been incinerated. To even suggest a parallel is to wholly misunderstand and trivialize the Holocaust experience. More should be expected from presumably feeling and compassionate "Artists." Just as more should be expected from COSMEP, an organization ostensibly committed to humane

*Reprinted from* Technicalities, *v. 5, no. 6 (June 1985), p. 13, by permission of M.E. Sharpe, Inc., Armonk NY 10504.*

values and elemental decency, which published a full-page Truth Missions'
ad in its latest *Catalogue*. Not only did the ad promote a blatantly anti-
Semitic work, but the main "business" of Truth Missions — the erstwhile
"small press" — is to propagate the notion that no Holocaust ever happened,
that there were no millions of dead and degraded. Asked at its recent St.
Paul conference to adopt civilized guidelines that would bar anti-Semitic,
racist, and sexist material from future catalogs, COSMEP refused. So its next
catalog may well serve, like this one, as a marketing vehicle for neo-Nazis
and anti-Semites. A tribute, perhaps, to "free speech." But not to human
dignity. Nor to social responsibility.

Undoubtedly good people, the guest editorial writers. Same for COSMEP.
Yet, like Brand, "I wonder whose side they're on."

SHALOM!

# TECHNOLOGY, HUMANISM, AND CIVIL LIBERTIES: A REVIEW

Oboler, Eli M. *To Free the Mind: Libraries, Technology, and Intellectual Freedom*. Littleton, Colo.: Libraries Unlimited, 1983. 124pp. $15.00. LC 83-19889. ISBN 0-87287-325-0.

We will seize Amerika's technology and use it to build a nation based on love and respect for all life.

Our new society is not about the power of a few men but the right of all humans, animals, and plants to play out their natural roles in harmony.

We will build our communities to reflect the beauty inside us.

People all over the world are fighting to keep Amerika from turning their countries into parking lots![1]

Disregard the ISBN number and price. Because this book isn't worth buying.

Although the late champion of intellectual freedom and library humanism argues passionately for making information as widely and freely available as possible, and despite his laudable recognition that too often $ = access (with the corollary that fees represent barriers to getting information), there's just not enough grist nor breadth to repay either the purchase cost or even the time spent reading. And beyond that, the tome is a poor example of bookmaking.

Essentially, this is a collection of short literature-surveys on topics like micrographics, utilities, CAI, privacy, and copyright, each overview mingled with personal remarks rendered in a frequently verbose, "talky," cliche-larded, and pedantic style (e.g., "may I add," "as we all know," "to be willing and able to do so," "haruspication"). Most of the treated subjects seem worth examining, but the treatment itself so often consists of excessive quotation, pedestrian comment, and repeated homilies that ultimately the whole work becomes a tedious parade of platitudes and paraphrases. Further, many truly

*An earlier, truncated version of this review appeared in* Technical Services Quarterly, *Fall 1986, pp. 116–18.*

relevant issues go unnoticed. And toward some grave matters the approach is at best superficial and at worst inaccurate.

A few specifics:

• Questionable, if not naive, assumptions or claims pass unchallenged: e.g., the prediction that "every home [will have] its own [electronic] access to practically everything" (page 5). AFDC households? Unemployed steelworkers? Seniors living on Social Security checks?

• Librarian-dependence is rightly considered as something to be avoided or at least minimized, yet there's no admission that online database searching—surely a major aspect of the new technology—is likely to reintroduce or reinforce such dependence. Additionally, and of clear "intellectual freedom" import, there's no characterization of the online databases and indexing services themselves as largely "mainstream" or elitist in scope: i.e., likely to constrict rather than expand the desired diversity of viewpoint, fact, and analysis. Nor does Oboler indicate the positive, countervailing potential of silicon-chip technology. (Says Steve Johnson: "For community organizations, online databases like those offered through DIALOG may only abstract a thin slice of the information a community organization desires. For example, very few data bases contain information on what librarians call 'fugitive literature,' material prepared by non-standard publishers, such as community groups themselves. With good microcomputer technology and relatively inexpensive ways to communicate data, community groups themselves can become providers for a database, working by themselves or in consort with others. Again, all through the electronic medium.")[2]

• There's no intimation of how technology might be—but largely isn't—utilized to enhance bibliographic access by such means as contemporizing subject headings and permitting abundant, even "transparent," cross-references. (Some libraries already have the powerful capacity to instantly transform all NEAR EAST to MIDDLE EAST forms. But they *don't do it!*) Nor is there an understanding of how—particularly in the case of ISBD—technology may be invoked as the reason for actually polluting and mystifying bibliographic records.

• While not strictly an "intellectual freedom" concern, certainly the real and probable effects of technology on library workers merited a little attention from someone widely respected as a humanist. But there's no mention of VDT hazards, technological unemployment, or such other possible outcomes of library automation as the computerized surveillance of data entry operators and increasing monotonization of clerical work.

• The author doubtless appreciates the economic and political dimensions of "information technology," but nowhere really explores the realities of communication development and control—e.g., the initial R & D on computers for purely military purposes—failing even to cite the paramount authority in this realm, Herbert Schiller.

• There's no acknowledgment of how automated catalogs, as one example of techno-progress, may actually frustrate some library users, especially the technically *il*literate. For instance, people who don't know how to use microfiche readers or balk at terminals may completely lose access to the catalog without deliberate and special instruction.

 • Unfortunately like many other intellectual freedom "purists," Oboler handles certain events and controversies in a blatantly lopsided, unfair way, exemplified here by: (a) blanketly attributing censorious motives and objectives to opponents of ALA's ostensibly "First Amendment" film, *The Speaker,* and (b) utterly misrepresenting the Third World rationale for a New World Information Order, as well as overlooking serious economic and political obstacles to the so-called "free flow of information" that, in effect, render it the "free flow of *Western* information" transmitted by and for multinational corporations and Euro-American governments. (Lee Regan writes: "The present information order, like the economic system, is chiefly vertically structured: North over South, rich over poor, educated over illiterate, experts over ordinary people. The assumption behind the new order is that horizontal relationships should replace the vertical ones. The distinction between communication as a human right and social good, and communication as a marketable commodity to be packaged and sold for personal profit is basic to the NWIO rationale.")[3]

 • "Ibid.'s" and brief bibliographic notes occupy an exorbitant amount of space.

 • The six-page index: (a) contains no items cited in notes or the bibliography; (b) furnishes no helpful "see" references (e.g., from "Talloires Declaration" to "Declaration of Talloires"); and (c) totally ignores a host of mentioned topics, persons, and groups, including no entries, e.g., for NASA (page 13), nuclear power (page 7), the atom bomb (pages 6–7), Nixon (pages 4, 6), union-busting (page 6), Luddism (page 87), Orwell (page 6), photocopying (page 11), the American Electronics Association (page 81), post-industrial society, or F.W. Lancaster (the last two appearing several times in the text).

 • Oboler alludes to adverse civil liberties consequences of nuclear power, but strangely misses the far greater, indeed overriding, threat posed to library collections and clients by nuclear holocaust.

The two concluding paragraphs on page 84, which state the "Oboler Utopia," qualify as the most inspiring and illuminating passages in the book. However, two paragraphs don't justify a $15 tab.

The impact of new technology on libraries and information access desperately needed a book-length examination, particularly from a humanistic standpoint. It still does.

## NOTES

1. Nancy Kurshan, Howie Reis and the 2nd National Yip Collective, "We Will Make Our New Nation Fit for Living Things," in *Blacklisted News, Secret History. . . From Chicago, '68 to 1984* (New York: Bleecker Publishing, 1983), p. 515.

2. "Community Applications of Information and Communication Technology," *Librarians for Social Change*, v. 11, no. 3 (1983), p. 12. See also my "Space Age Hardware, Stone Age Data," *Technicalities*, v. 1, no. 12 (Nov. 1981), pp. 11-12.

3. "The New World Information Order," *SRRT Newsletter*, no. 73 (Sept. 1984), p. 5.

# CREATIONISM

# NOT-SO-HIDDEN AGENDA

Why do Creationists

- try so hard to get "equal time" (with evolution) in biology classes and textbooks?
- train and certify teachers for guerrilla operations in public schools?
- contest evolution-teaching as a "civil rights" violation?
- badger libraries, especially in schools, to stock Creationist material and legitimate it — through classification and subject cataloging — as "science"?

Curtis Sewell, an electronics engineer at Lawrence Livermore Laboratory who teaches "scientific creationism" for Trinity Baptist Church, candidly told an interviewer:

> It is true that a belief in creationism will never save someone. Yet it will open the door to the possibility of a person's receiving Christ as his savior. After all, if a person deeply believes in evolutionism, then he also believes that the Bible cannot be true, and is thus not receptive to the gospel of salvation — it must be a fairy tale. This is the factor that leads most college students to reject their Christian raising. [*Valley Times,* August 11, 1984, p. 5A.]

*Reprinted from* Technicalities, *v. 5, no. 2 (Feb. 1985), p. 7, by permission of M.E. Sharpe, Inc., Armonk NY 10504.*

# GIMME THAT
# OLD TIME RELIGION

In its "Echoes: From the Editor's Mail," the September 1984 *Bible-Science Newsletter* (6245 Newton Ave. S., Richfield MN 55423) ran this editorial paragraph:

> In the June *Pulse* column we mentioned Sanford Berman's suggestion that the Library of Congress cataloging system was inadequate for books of creation science since it lists such books as science. Berman, head cataloger for the Hennepin County (Minneapolis) Library system, and an anti-creationist, suggested that Library of Congress classifications for books on creation science should be ignored and the books placed into the category of "specific topics in Christian theology." Clayton D. Loughran wrote us in response to these comments. Loughran has an M.S. in library science and has served in the National Library of Medicine as well as several university libraries over his career.

That prefaced Loughran's missive:

> We in the profession swear by the expert classification and cataloguing of the Library of Congress, trust it and never alter it. It is definitely superior to the Dewey Decimal classification system: a first-class system like the Enoch Pratt Library in Baltimore, taught us as a model of public library administration, has gone to huge expense to *re*classify its collection according to Library of Congress procedure. This at a time when salaries eat up an institution's budget, books cost $15 or $20 for a dime novel, and the processes involved in accessioning, cataloguing, labeling, etc., add certainly $5 to $7 per book in labor costs.
>
> Do not surrender, do not let Berman off the hook. He is a public servant and not entitled to inflict his private views on the library he serves.

Well, HCL's in *Minnetonka,* not *Minneapolis;* many libraries regularly truncate or otherwise alter LC-assigned classification numbers; and I have never publicly compared the LC and Dewey schemes (although I *do* think it silly

*Reprinted from* Technicalities, *v. 5, no. 2 (Feb. 1985), p. 7, by permission of M.E. Sharpe, Inc., Armonk NY 10504.*

and irresponsible for a public library to "convert" from Dewey to LC, as many did during a lemming-like hysteria some 10 years ago). But apart from that misinformation, the larger allegations are either wrong or unhelpfully simplistic. So to clarify matters, here's an "Open Letter on the Classification and Subject Cataloging of Creationist Literature":

1. Since our library doesn't use Library of Congress Classification (LCC), I'm not intimately familiar with that system. However, these are facts:

• The Dewey Decimal Classification, employed by most school and public libraries, as well as many smaller academic institutions, specifies a discrete notation — 231.765 — for "Creation" within a sequence devoted to "Specific topics in Christian doctrinal theology." Further, a scope-note declares: "Including relation of scientific and Christian viewpoints." (In all likelihood, LCC contains a comparable notation within its Christian theology schedule, probably "BS651-652," judging from the below-quoted LCSH entry.)

• The Library of Congress subject heading list (LCSH), which serves as the basis or authority for assigning subject headings throughout most of the English-speaking library world, contains this entry/descriptor:

Creationism *(BS651-652)*

Here are entered works on the doctrine that the universe was created by God out of nothing in the initial seven days of time and that all biological species were created rather than evolving from preexisting types through modifications in successive generations.

   x Scientific creationism
  xx Bible and evolution
     Creation
     Evolution — Religious aspects
     Modernist-fundamentalist controversy

To interpret slightly: x = "see" reference (i.e., a cross-reference should appear in the catalog *from* "Scientific creationism" to the actually utilized term CREATIONISM), and xx = "see also from" reference (e.g., BIBLE AND EVOLUTION. *See also* CREATIONISM).

• At the Library of Congress, the source of most libraries' "cataloging copy" (whether in the form of Cataloging-in-Publication entries, online MARC records, or LC cards), the Decimal Classification Division (DCD), headed by John P. Comaromi, assigns Dewey numbers to new works, while the Subject Cataloging Division (SCD), supervised by Mary Kay Pietris, assigns both LCC numbers and LC subject headings.

2. A central principle of classification is that the assigned classification number should truly reflect what the particular work is about: i.e., what subject it deals with. Accordingly, a work that deals mainly, if not wholly, with the subject of evolution should be classed in the "Evolution" number (e.g., "575" in Dewey), no matter how foolish or unscientific the content or approach. As a result, Creationist-published, religiously inspired critiques

of evolution will cohabit on library shelves with bona fide scientific treatments of the same topic. So, for instance, assuming that Duane Gish's *Evolution: The Fossils Say No!* primarily addresses the subject of evolution — regardless of how inadequately — it merits an "Evolution" classification number.

The same principle, if applied evenhandedly, will mandate the classification of works primarily espousing, critiquing, or describing "Creationism" — again, regardless of attitude or provenance — in the specified "Creationism" number (e.g., "231.765" in Dewey).

To state the obvious: Not *all* works produced *by* Creationists will necessarily be classed in a "Creationism" number, just as not all material authored or published by Evolutionists will merit an "Evolution" notation:

• The Gish tome, although written and published by Creationists, should probably be classed in the Evolution number;

• Ashley Montagu's Oxford University Press anthology, *Science and Creationism,* although authored by Evolutionists, should be classed in "Creationism" (because that's the key topic it addresses);

• *What Is Creation Science?*, jointly authored by Henry M. Morris and Gary E. Parker, and issued by Creation-Life Publishers, deserves classing in "Creationism" (e.g., 231.765), inasmuch as it explicitly and overwhelming deals with "creation science."

*The classification* problem *is that the Library of Congress has unfortunately classified Creationism/Evolution materials in an inconsistent — and frequently mistaken — fashion.* Montagu's collection, e.g., was classed in "Evolution," despite its critical emphasis on "Creationism," while the Morris/Parker book went into "501," the notation for "Philosophy and theory of science"!! And Roland Mushat Frye's 1983 anthology, *Is God a Creationist? The Religious Case Against Creation-Science,* emerged from DCD with "213," the Dewey number for "Creation" within the "Natural religion" sequence, which — while surely more appropriate than any notation derived from the 500 (Science) schedule — nonetheless misrepresented the content: essentially an attack on the Bible-based "creationism" espoused by fundamentalist Christians (not "natural religionists").

3. The practice of subject cataloging — i.e., assigning subject headings or subject access points to a given work — ordinarily permits the assignment of more than one heading to the same work, if appropriate. (In other words, the constraint imposed on classifiers — to only assign *one* number or shelf "address" — doesn't apply.) As already noted, both EVOLUTION and CREATIONISM are available for use by LC subject catalogers.

*Again, as with classification, the* problem *is that the Library of Congress has unfortunately not always assigned the appropriate headings to particular titles and often assigns too few descriptors to fully and honestly represent subject content and permit useful subject retrieval.* Montagu's anthology, e.g., got *no* subject heading for CREATIONISM. And neither did the Morris/Parker volume, whose very title announces its subject: *What Is Creation Science?*

# "IN THE BEGINNING":
# THE CREATIONIST AGENDA

Some people think God made the universe in six days and personally handcrafted each plant and animal specie. They think so because that's what it says in Genesis, the Old Testament story. And they regard that story as the literal Word of God.

They also believe in a "young earth," probably not more than 10,000 years old. And Noah's Ark. And the "special," sudden creation of human beings during that same week — not very long ago — that God created algae, amoeba, and chimpanzees.

They should, of course, be completely free to believe these things. And to say what they believe. But "Creationists" do much more than merely hold such beliefs. Or express them. For instance:

In Arkansas, Louisiana, Minnesota, Tennessee, and at least 17 other states, laws have been proposed requiring that Creationism be taught in public schools — i.e., in public school *science* classes — as a competing "theory" with Evolution. Creationists lobby at the national level for passage of an "Act To Protect Academic Freedom and To Prevent Federal Censorship in Scientific Inquiry Funded with Federal Tax Monies" that would mandate research, curriculum development, and museum exhibit funding for *both* origin "models." (For statute texts, together with Judge William R. Overton's 1982 opinion on the Arkansas bill's unconstitutionality, see Peter Zetterberg's *Evolution Versus Creationism: the Public Education Controversy,* Oryx Press, 1983, pp. 385–429.)

The Fall 1984 issue of *Creation/Evolution* (p. 52) reported the latest developments in what might have been a protracted Louisiana court battle. In the meantime, though, a federal District Court in New Orleans declared the law unconstitutional and the 5th U.S. Circuit Court of Appeals upheld that ruling, stating that "the act's intended effect is to discredit evolution by counterbalancing its teaching at every turn with the teaching of creationism, a religious belief." (Source: *Herald* [Livermore CA], July 9, 1985, p. 3.)

*Reprinted with permission from* Library Journal, *Oct. 15, 1985, pp. 31-4.*

Creationists try to foist the same "two-theory" approach on textbook publishers; or, failing that, demand the total elimination of "evolution" from biology texts, this most notably in Texas, a major market whose buying policies — heavily influenced by the fundamentalist Gablers — impact upon school districts everywhere. (For more details on the Texas situation, see, for instance, People For the American Way's special, two-page report, *The Texas Connection: Countering the Textbook Censorship Crusade* [1982], and "The Textbook Selection Process in Texas: Group Works To Improve Selection Process/Far Right Works To Turn Back the Clock," *Interracial Books for Children Bulletin,* v. 14, no. 5 [1983], pp. 14-17. But Ronnie J. Hastings, a Texas science teacher, in two *Skeptical Inquirer* articles claims that matters have improved ["Evolution and Science Education in Texas: Two Victories After a Winter of Discontent," Summer 1984, pp. 290-292, and "New Biology Texts for Texas Contain Material on Evolution," Fall 1984, p. 10]. Thomas H. Jukes recounts "Creationist efforts to censor textbooks and harass writers on evolution" in his "Creationist Challenge to Science," in the March 29, 1984, issue of *Nature* [pp. 398-400], while the March and August 1983 "Consumer, Beware!" columns in *Technicalities* deal with censorship by two particular presses, Laidlaw Brothers and Holt, Rinehart & Winston ["Info Indicators," p. 7 and "Capitulating to the Yahoos," pp. 15-16]. However, a November 13, 1984, letter to *People For*'s Barbara Parker from Herbert R. Adams, Laidlaw Brothers' new president, announced "significant changes," including "substantial coverage of evolution" in biology texts. For an official version of the "two-theory" approach, see "Statement on Origins: Christian Educator and Parents Association of Minnesota," *Bible-Science Newsletter,* February 1984, p. 14. Incidentally, the Gabler and fundamentalist influence on Texas textbooks may well have contributed to that state's poor scholastic showing. In a recent Department of Education survey, Texas came out *below average* in college entrance exam scores as well as high school graduation rates.)

Creationists induce local school districts to add creationism to the science curriculum, as in Prescott, Arizona, where, in late 1984, the Mayer School District board directed that the "theory of creation" be taught in science classes from sixth grade through high school, using textbooks produced by Christian Heritage College. (Source: *Prescott Courier,* November 13, 1984.)

Creationists initiate "civil rights" court suits, arguing that their children's "religious liberty" is being violated by compulsory school exposure to evolution (which contradicts their religious beliefs) without complementary instruction in Creationism (which accords with those beliefs). In Iowa, for example, teachers and superintendents have been threatened with having their certification revoked for "violating students' civil rights," while school board members who "allow discrimination" face removal from office by the District Court. (Robert Schadewald furnishes details on this novel approach in "New Creationist Strategy," *Minnesota Skeptics Newsletter* [549 Turnpike Rd., Golden

Valley MN 55416], August 1984, p. 4. So does editor Fred Edwords in the Fall 1984 issue of *Creation/Evolution,* pp. 51–52. The sidebar quoting the April 28, 1984, *Des Moines Register* concerns a recent Iowa case involving a whole school district.)

Creationists train and certify Creationist biology teachers — at institutions like Tim LaHaye's Christian Heritage College and Jerry Falwell's Liberty University (formerly Liberty Baptist College) — for essentially "undercover" activity in public schools. In fact, the nearly 1000 fundamentalist teachers who belong to NACE — the National Association of Christian Educators — "unabashedly," according to Fred Edwords, "vow to teach Christian fundamentalism in public schools wherever they can find an opening," and especially target gifted students.

This clandestine teaching has taken place in Michigan, Wisconsin, California, New York, and elsewhere, with perhaps the greatest concentration in California's Santa Clara Valley and San Francisco Bay Area. As declared in late 1983 by NACE's national leaders, the organization's next tactic will be the formation of parent pressure groups:

> We have now begun our campaign to start a Christian parents' organization called "Citizens for Excellence in Education." Our goal is to have committees in all 16,000 school districts in America. We can totally change our schools through these parent groups, who will influence all our school boards and bring back our Christian values and morality, and a national faith in God.

(Sources: Frederick Edwords, "Creation/Evolution Update: the Battle Goes Underground," *Humanist,* September/October 1984, p. 38, and Fall 1984 *Creation/Evolution,* pp. 53–54. Also: Robert L. Simonds' *Communicating a Christian World View in the Classroom: a Manual,* issued by NACE in 1983, and the group's two periodicals, both noted under "Resources.")

Creationists attempt to pack libraries — especially in schools — with Creationist materials, harassing those that either don't meet their quotas or stock too many occult, non–Christian, or other unsavory, irreligious items. Still another approach is to demand the removal from libraries and classrooms of works that "dogmatically support evolution"; for example, Helena Curtis' *Biology,* a textbook, and PBS' *Life on Earth* program. (For further data, see "Four More Library Surveys," *Bible-Science Newsletter,* August 1984, p. 13; *Creation/Evolution Newsletter,* March/April 1984, p. 3; "News Briefs," *Creation/Evolution,* Fall 1984, pp. 50–52; and *Des Moines Register* sidebar. Also: Bruce A. Schuman's hypothetical case, "A Matter of Balance," in which "Creationists protest the library's perceived bias in favor of the evolutionist argument," *River Bend Revisited,* Oryx Press, 1984, pp. 100–102.)

Creationists want Creationist literature to be considered bona fide "science" and thus classified by libraries in the Dewey 500s rather than in 231.765, the notation specified for "Creation" within the sequence devoted to

"Specific topics in Christian doctrinal theology," and would probably like to substitute SCIENTIFIC CREATIONISM or CREATION SCIENCE for the current Library of Congress subject heading, CREATIONISM, the "science" again lending respectability to the topic. (For extensive data and citations on the library/Creationist nexus, with an emphasis on cataloging and classification, see "Should Special Interest Groups Be Allowed to Classify Books?" *Bible-Science Newsletter,* June 1984, p. 17, and Clayton D. Loughran's follow-up letter, September 1984; "Library Issues," *Creation/Evolution Newsletter,* July/August 1984, pp. 13–15; two *Technicalities* columns, both titled "Gimme That Old Time Religion," June 1984, p. 10, and August 1984, p. 7; and "Pseudoscience, Creationism and the Library," by Rice University librarians James C. Thompson and Kay A. Flowers, in the November 1984 *Catholic Library World,* pp. 176–179.)

This nationwide, well-financed Creationist crusade is not simply about fundamentalist children's "rights" or quibbles over The Flood and Garden of Eden. It is a deliberate effort to publicly legitimize a central doctrine, a key dogma, of Christian Fundamentalism and, by so doing, promote and expand the entire movement, leading ultimately to a Fundamentalist America: a theocratic state and thoroughly "Christianized" society founded on Biblical literalism and viewing nonbelievers as pitiable, if not despicable, heretics, as unredeemed, Christ-denying, second-class citizens. Says Anthony Holz in the October 26, 1984, *American Jewish World* (p. 5):

> Current efforts to reintroduce prayer in public schools and to control what people see, read, or do in privacy illustrate the increasing urge to Christianize this country. We see this in attempts to incorporate into our laws principles and values that are basically Christian (and not necessarily shared by other faiths).... Depending on how they view the founding of this country, the would-be Christianizers can be easily divided into two groups. The first perceives America as having been founded Christian, and therefore as always having been a Christian country. The second realizes that America was not founded as a Christian state but contends it should have been. Consequently, that group considers it a religious and moral duty to Christianize the nation and thereby remedy what they see as a grave defect.... Liberal religion, Jewish or otherwise, can exist only in a pluralistic democracy. The basic principle of liberal religion, that all people have the ultimate right to decide for themselves on all matters of belief and value, can be realized only in a society that is free, nontheocratic, and nonauthoritarian.

In short, the Creationist onslaught must be seen as one aspect of the larger New Right/Christian Right offensive, a danger not solely to good science education (precisely at a time when schools are being exhorted to produce more and better scientists and engineers), but also to church-state separation, religious pluralism, intellectual freedom, and elemental democracy.

## Ongoing Resources

1. Sanford Berman, Head Cataloger, Hennepin Country Library, 12601 Ridgedale Drive, Minnetonka MN 55343-5648; (612) 541-8570. Authority on library-connected matters.

2. *Bible-Science Newsletter,* 2911 East 42nd Street, Minneapolis MN 55408. m. $17. Organ of Bible-Science Association. Important for learning not only *what* they're doing or plan to do, but also *why.*

3. *Creation/Evolution,* P.O. Box 146, Amherst Branch, Buffalo NY 14226-0146. q. $9. Editor: Fred Edwords. Deals mainly with legal, teaching, and science aspects of Creationism. "Major source of ammunition for debaters, lawyers, lobbyists, teachers, and concerned citizens."

4. *Creation/Evolution Newsletter,* National Center for Science Education, Box 32, Concord College, Athens WV 24712. bi-m. $5. Editor: Karl D. Fezer. Accents Creationist ploys and organized counterattacks by the scientific, educational, and civil libertarian communities. Combined subscription to both *C/E* and *C/E Newsletter:* $12.

Another useful NCSE publication: *Reviews of Thirty-One Creationist Books* (1984), a 71-page compendium edited by Stan Weinberg that "covers the major works in the creationist canon, critically but fairly." Price: $5.50, from NCSE, Dept. B, 156 East Alta Vista, Ottumwa IA 52501.

Sample passages from Karl D. Fezer's review of Davis A. Young's *Christianity and the Age of the Earth* and Henry M. Morris' *Science, Scripture, and the Young Earth:*

> One must respect Young's work. If one wishes to give students a book written from the creationist point of view that is timely, candid, and scholarly, this is the book. Young, and others who share his views, can contribute significantly to educating the public, and especially their fellow evangelicals, on the nature of that limited enterprise called science. Morris, on the other hand, clearly does let his religious views distort his attempts to reason scientifically. His enterprise is quite different from science. Much of the creation/evolution controversy would vanish if he and his fellow "scientific creationists" frankly acknowledged this....

5. *Education Newsline,* Box 3200, Costa Mesa CA 92628. bi-m. $15. Editor: Eric J. Buehrer. Joint organ of the National Association of Christian Educators (NACE) and Citizens for Excellence in Education (CEE), whose aim is to "change America's school system by Christian teachers from within and Christian parents from without." Contains annotated lists of resources to support anti-"humanist," pro–Christian curricula and counseling, and propounds techniques for infusing public school classroom subjects with fundamentalist dogma, including creationism.

The premier (February/March 1985) issue, for instance, featured this review of John N. Moore's *How To Teach Origins (Without ACLU Interference),* a 1983 Mott Media title:

Focused specifically on teaching creationism in the public schools, Moore, prof. emeritaus [sic] of natural science at Michigan State Univ., provides sound analysis, diagrams for teaching aids, discussion questions, classroom projects or individual assignments, an annotated bibiliography [sic] of creationist books, and addresses where further materials can be obtained. Moore also provides the legal foundations for teaching creationism.

For $32, NACE/CEE members receive not only *Education Newsline,* but also the quarterly *Christians in Education* and "free info. packages on legal briefs and education programs." Incidentally, Simonds' earlier-noted "Manual," which only costs $5, includes "A Summary of Scientific Evidence for Creation," as well as this statement, captioned "Christ's Creation Vs. Man's Evolution":

The Christian accepts the Biblical account that God created all things — man, animals, plants, planets, the universe, and all matter. The secular humanist accepts a notion proposed by Darwin, that all things exist as a natural evolvement from something which always existed. Life sprang forth from inorganic mass by an explosion or accident of nature. To the secular scientist, material or energy, shaped by chance, without a plan or a planner behind it, is our only reality.

6. People for the American Way, 1424 16th St. NW, Suite 601, Washington DC 20036. Anti–New Right organization founded by Norman Lear. Produces TV spots, print ads, films, posters, a *Quarterly Report,* issue papers, and citizen action guides for combating not only school, library, and textbook censorship, but also attempts to mandate prayer and creationism in public schools.

7. *Skeptical Inquirer,* Box 229, Central Park Station, Buffalo NY 14215. q. $16.50. Editor: Kendrick Frazier. Organ of CSICOP (Committee for the Scientific Investigation of Claims of the Paranormal). Often runs Creationist-related news and articles; e.g., in "The Creationist Threat: Science Finally Awakens" (Spring 1982, pp. 2–6), Frazier details the Creationist offensive, including such "terrorist tactics" as "a call by the Institute for Creation Research to have members turn in the names of teachers who are teaching evolution or preventing the teaching of creationism"; surveys the counterattack being mounted by scientists, educators, and civil libertarians; and concludes with this observation by Isaac Asimov: "With creationism in the saddle, American science will wither. We will raise a generation of ignoramuses ill-equipped to run the industry of tomorrow, much less to generate the new advances of the days after tomorrow."

# RELIGION AND/OR SCIENCE

Gunther (Letters, *Library Journal,* January 1986, page 10) and Rush (page 8) variously accuse me of advocating the exclusion of Creationist material from libraries and their exclusive classification — or segregation — in Dewey's 231.765 notation. (Of course, if truly excluded, there'd be nothing to classify!) As it happens, two other people wrote me directly, making similar allegations, one also implying that because of my baneful influence Hennepin County Library probably doesn't stock *any* Creationist works. My April 1986 "Consumer, Beware!" column in *Technicalities* will fully reprint those two missives, together with a reply which states, in part:

> Nowhere in that article, "In the Beginning: the Creationist Agenda" (*LJ*, October 15, pp. 31–34) did I advocate censorship of Creationist literature. On the contrary, the report cited several instances of Creationist-inspired textbook tampering and flagrant attempts to remove "from libraries and classrooms ... works that 'dogmatically support evolution.'" Further, the implication that Creationist materials have been deliberately excluded from the library where I work is at once unfounded and insulting. In fact, as these [reproduced] entries from the HCL Catalog demonstrate, the Creationist viewpoint is well represented — and I personally "confess" to having recommended a number of pro-Creationist items myself.

Among the reproduced entries are two by Henry M. Morris and two by Duane Gish, both leading Creationists. Interestingly, all four critics conveniently ignored my charge that Creationists themselves practice still another form of censorship: attempting to "pack libraries" and classrooms with the dozens of books and pamphlets produced mainly by Creation Life Publishers and the Bible-Science Association (see my June 1984 *Technicalities* column for examples). Indeed, a new ploy in that campaign — as openly related by Luther D. Sunderland in the February 1986 *Bible Science Newsletter* — is to flood school libraries with donations.

To cope with these perhaps irrelevant and unwanted gifts, school librarians should develop selection and gift policies that unequivocally declare what is and isn't appropriate to their collections....

*Reprinted with permission from* Library Journal, *March 15, 1986, pp. 6–7.*

Finally, an update: Although two federal courts declared Louisiana's "balanced treatment law" unconstitutional, State Attorney General William Guste on December 2, 1985, declared he "would request a U.S. Supreme Court review of the lower court's decree and ask for a reversal of an earlier summary judgment made against the state." So it's not over yet on the judicial front.

# ANOTHER LETTER
# THAT WASN'T/GIMME THAT
# OLD TIME RELIGION
# (GRAND FINALE)

This missive, sent to *Library Journal* on February 22, 1986, never appeared in Bowker's redesigned rag:

Dear Colleagues,

Joseph McDonald and George A. Mindeman ("Letters," Feb. 1, 1986) both minimize the Creationist threat to science education and church-state separation. McDonald says "Creationism . . . is a fringe," while Mindeman sarcastically exclaims, "Ye gads! Creationism/Fundamentalism is relentlessly marching on. Who can save us now?" Well, Chris McGowan addressed precisely this issue in the "Afterword" to his 1984 Prometheus Books title, *In the Beginning . . . a Scientist shows why the Creationists Are Wrong:*

> The creation-evolution controversy must rank fairly low in our scale of priorities, well below our concerns for the economy, and further still below our concerns over the nuclear threat. It would be all too easy to shrug it off as an issue of marginal importance, an issue that will probably all blow over in any case. But I would like to suggest that it is not such a small issue, and that it really is not going to go away. I am not unduly troubled that my two daughters are not being taught about evolution in their science classrooms, but I am concerned that they might be exposed to a hodgepodge of ignorance and half-truths presented to them as a "scientific" alternative to evolution. As I see it, the evolution issue is just the thin edge of the wedge. If creationism is successfully legislated into our school system, what will come next? Why should the fundamentalists stop short at biology? Why should they not also have the right to teach their beliefs in a 10,000-year-old universe and in light rays that distort to fit the "facts." Should the creationists

*Reprinted from* Technicalities, *v. 6, no. 11 (Nov. 1986), p. 13, by permission of M.E. Sharpe, Inc., Armonk NY 10504.*

have their way, I believe we would see science revert back to the mystical art form that it was during the dark ages.

Monthly letters to NACE/CEE members from President Robert L. Simonds provide further evidence that the danger is not only real, but extends well beyond Creationism. Simonds' February 1986 missive, for instance, celebrates the CEE-demanded scrapping of a drug and alcohol abuse program in one Washington State school district, continued CEE opposition to *The Learning Tree* in another district ("a battle for decency and the preservation of man's right to believe in God"), and the election of CEE candidates to a third district's school board, where they presumably will escalate the battle against "power-crazed unions (NEA and all state affiliates) and secular humanist purveyors of atheism." No danger, huh?

Charlotte M. Gunther ("Letters," Jan. 1986) mused that "perhaps Berman is unaware that there are people of great intelligence and understanding in all fields of science who believe in Special Creation." Sorry to disillusion her, but Henry P. Cole and Eugenie C. Scott have shown, in 2 separate reports, that "scientific creationists" have failed to publish studies "that support their basic assumptions and concepts," that contributions to "mainline" scientific journals "were rejected due to poor scholarship, with editors commenting that the articles appeared to have been written by laymen rather than professional scientists," and that "outside of creationist outlets, there is no 'scientific creationism.'" Additionally, Ronald H. Pine, in the Fall 1984 *Creation/Evolution,* exploded the contention that bona fide "scientists" promote Creationism, concluding that

> Some scientific creationists have never been scientists. Some were actual scientists for a period of time, but haven't been since. Others may play the game of science when they're working on their specialty, and even do it well enough to make a living at it, and then do pseudoscience in their off hours. To the extent that they do the latter, they are pseudoscientists.

# NO COMMENT

This missive, dated October 28, 1985, came in the mail with a legible signature and complete address, both of which are being omitted to spare the writer needless embarrassment:

I read with interest your article in the October 15 *Library Journal.* You sound quite alarmed, as though decadent, pagan America was in grave danger of being forcibly "Christianized." Well, relax. No doubt the drug and alcohol abuse, the mindless materialism, the child prostitution, the billion-dollar pornography industry, the battered children, in short, all the fruits of a Godless, valueless society will continue. Someday you will have to write an article for *LJ* demonstrating how the Enlightenment philosopher's boundless confidence in human nature has been borne out by the 20th Century. (By the way, two can play the text-book tinkering game. But if the group demanding a rewrite meets *LJ*'s approval, it's called "consciousness raising," not "censorship.")

*Reprinted from* Technicalities, *v. 6, no. 5 (May 1986), p. 15, by permission of M.E. Sharpe, Inc., Armonk NY 10504.*

# INTERVIEW

# ALTERNATIVE PERSPEC-TIVES: A CONVERSATION WITH SANDY BERMAN

## CONDUCTED BY JIM DWYER

*Dwyer:* Are you now or have you ever been a Sandynista?

*Berman:* With a small "y," yes. In fact, since birth. Lately it developed that Karl Nyren, writing in *Library Hotline,* referred to Hennepin County Library catalogers as "freedom fighters in the trenches." Well, it struck one or two of my colleagues that the term "freedom fighters," inasmuch as President Reagan often invokes it in happy reference to the Nicaraguan "Contras"—that pack of murderers, rapists, and drug smugglers—didn't seem the right kind of appellation for us. Once this little nugget appeared in the press and got bandied about in the cataloging section, someone said, "No, we're not freedom fighters, we're Sandynistas," spelled as you can imagine. That turned into a letter to Mr. Nyren correcting his original nomenclature, and that too got published in *Library Hotline.* So the matter is now straightened out. It wasn't my idea at all, but I confess I like it.

*Dwyer:* You've always been a controversial character, and I know that sometimes you've run into a certain amount of opposition. As an example, can you tell us about the process of getting your first book, *Prejudices and Antipathies,* published?

*Berman:* I claim no initial responsibility for it. The truth is that before that project I never thought I'd write a book. Didn't think I *could.* Well, I was wrong. Every new Assistant Librarian at the University of Zambia, where I was working in 1969, started with a couple months' apprenticeship in the cataloging department. It was then, in the course of strictly, uncritically, and even slavishly applying Library of Congress subject headings, that I discovered a number of anomalies. Worse than anomalies, a number of

*Reprinted from* Technicalities, *v. 6, no. 10 (Oct. 1986), pp. 3-9, by permission of M.E. Sharpe, Inc., Armonk NY 10504.*

grotesqueries. For instance, works on Black South Africans would regularly be assigned the heading *Kafirs.* All I had to do was ask a fellow cataloger, who happened to be from Swaziland, or another who was what South Africans call "Colored," what the hell "Kafir" meant. It was the equivalent of "nigger." So there I was in an independent, southern African country, a Third World country, and we were assigning a "nigger" heading which would be unacceptable even in the United States, to works about Africans — a word, a term, a name that none of us would ever say to either of these two co-workers from Swaziland and Capetown. So it was that kind of sensitization that prompted a short letter to *Library Journal* delicately implying, with four examples — *Native Races* being one of them, and the subhead, *Discovery and exploration* being another — that maybe something was rotten in LC-type subject cataloging. LC practice made it seem, for instance, that Victoria Falls had never been "discovered" until Europeans like Livingstone stumbled upon them. The local people, the Toka-Leya, can constantly hear the Falls. They've lived there for a lot longer than any Europeans, and had their own name for it, which I cited in that brief *LJ* letter. Well, I left it at that. That was as much at that point as I anticipated would come from this sensitization to Third World issues and how Western bias infused our major subject heading scheme. Then a letter arrived, unexpected, unsolicited, from an editor at ALA Publishing Services, whom I'm not going to name because I've since met him and he's a really decent guy, but he made a terrible mistake in this case. As I recall, he attached a photocopy of my missive and asked, "Sandy, you're not going to let it go at this, are you?" He then proceeded to suggest that maybe a whole book expanding upon bias and prejudice in the LC scheme would be appropriate and indicated a positive and explicit interest by ALA in publishing such a work. With the permission, bless him, of my boss, a "Brit" named Anthony Loveday, I broke my ass and after several months produced the manuscript for *Prejudices and Antipathies.* I shared some of the pieces along the way by mail with the ALA editor, who at first continued his encouragement, but ultimately found the text unacceptable for publication. There were some trivial objections about style and word usage, which I won't detail, but essentially ALA refused to print it because it was too critical — and this is almost an exact quote — of "such a venerable and respected institution" as the Library of Congress. Also, it was deemed "vituperative." So, since I wasn't prepared to change the basic tone and style and couldn't do anything about LC being such a "venerable institution," we mutually cancelled the contract. I then immediately submitted this very same unacceptable, vitriolic, disrespectful manuscript to Scarecrow Press where Eric Moon then presided, and it seemed, in retrospect, merely moments later that he replied, "Of course, we'll publish it. It looks like a landmark title to me." They had it out within five or six months.

   *Dwyer:* Surely with your success in publishing since then you haven't had any similar problems recently, have you?

*Berman:* Oh, have we! Jim Danky and I a couple of years ago decided that a complement, not competitor, to Bill Katz' annual, *The Best of Library Literature,* was in order. It would encompass not necessarily the "best" kind of literature, but certainly literature genuinely representing alternative viewpoints, or what some have called the "flip-side" of librarianship. In other words, the sort of viewpoints that can't be found readily nor regularly on the pages of *Wilson Library Bulletin, American Libraries,* and *Library Journal,* but may appear in some out-of-the-way sources not generally viewed by other colleagues, titles like LNAC *Almanac,* issued by an anti-nuclear library group; *Librarians for Social Change,* which itself is a truly "venerable" title from England; Noel Peattie's incomparable *Sipapu;* and *Women Library Workers Journal,* which I admit is indexed by *Library Literature,* unlike the other three, but probably doesn't circulate very widely. We knew from our own experience that there was really a lot of literature dealing with ethnic and women's library services, and with censorship from a slightly different angle than the Establishment approach represented by the IFC, Judy Krug, and First Amendment "purists." We knew there was material being published that was exciting, often even funny, that a lot of people weren't seeing, and that we desperately wanted to share because *we* were seeing it. So we put together the first anthology, called *Alternative Library Literature, 1982–83.* Oryx Press gladly accepted the idea and published without any trouble a very handsome volume illustrated with offbeat cartoons and including—if I say so myself—an excellent index. Anyway, that came out and was very well reviewed, but apparently its sales didn't satisfy Oryx. At any rate, they declined to continue publishing it, but didn't mind if somebody else picked it up, which seemed reasonable enough.

Jim and I then sought other publishers. We tried ALA, pointing out that it was one of their mandates as an organization to promote social responsibility but that their publications list didn't seem to reflect much social responsibility. This, we gently observed, would be an opportunity to meet that mandate. We got, "Oh, yes, social responsibility is a wonderful thing, but it doesn't seem to sell many copies." It was again a kind of a bottom-line argument, rather than emphasizing what might be good and needed in library literature. We tried something like four or five other publishers, getting the same kind of response, mostly "gee whiz, we think it's a nice idea, the first edition was sure swell, but we don't want to take a chance with it." Maybe they had other, unvoiced concerns. Who knows? Well, the last one we tried was McFarland & Company, a relative newcomer in library publishing, located in Jefferson, North Carolina. We had so little hope that this last chance would work that I just marked up an old cover letter like the one we'd sent to ALA, kind of shoddy looking, and sent it off with a few samples from the manuscript. We figured that it was a good idea, but one that just wasn't going to fly because the mood of the times was wrong and there did seem to be an economic factor working against us: small anticipated sales. Within two days, Robbie Franklin, president of McFarland, phoned in a state of what I can only call electric enthusiasm, which I hadn't experienced about a book project from anybody for a long, long time, and wanted to know whether we'd given the thing to any other publisher because he was prepared to grab it back if that were the case. Now, some months later, it's finally scheduled to appear in October or November with splendid illustrations by a local Minneapolis artist, Jackie Urbanovic, who was also featured in the first volume. We think it has some damn fine content, maybe even better than the first one, ranging from a right-on preface by Elliott Shore to a special section on the library/apartheid connection that's particularly rich in analysis, resources, and passion.

*Dwyer:* What would you say are your top priorities as a librarian?

*Berman:* It's very difficult for me, almost impossible at most times, to separate personal from professional and, I must add, from social and political. Now, others may say that I *ought* to be able to do that! I find it very hard. I'd prefer to be in this case a somewhat holistic person and I think that's what happens.

*Dwyer:* Might that be one of the problems with our society?

*Berman:* That could be, but I'm glad that you said it instead of me. The priorities for me in terms of what I do and what I'd also like to have an impact on are greater equity and a larger sense of social justice within librarianship. Put negatively, perhaps, but importantly: less mystification and less elitism. In other words, a greater openness, less hierarchy and "bossism," less secrecy and greater accessibility, both to ourselves as professionals, and to the materials and services that we're supposed to be providing everybody. I think we've got a long way to go on that.

*Dwyer:* Let's look on the other side of the bibliographic coin. In a 1985 ALA survey, 250 library leaders were asked to rank 16 areas of interest. Not surprisingly, legislation and access to information were ranked first and second. More interestingly, career development was seventh while literacy/illiteracy was fourteenth and international relations was a very distant last. In ranking 32 areas of action, promoting the importance of libraries to society was fourth and promoting equality of service to all groups, one of your main concerns, was eighth, yet removing economic barriers was twenty-eighth, promoting library services to the economically disadvantaged was twenty-ninth, removing physical barriers to the handicapped was thirtieth, and promoting library services to the elderly was, if you'll excuse the expression, dead last. What does this say about our leaders' priorities?

*Berman:* That they are ass-backwards. I don't know where to begin exactly, but let's select barriers, for instance, to poor people and ethnic minorities who by virtue of powerlessness and language may not readily access library services nor demand them. The upcoming *Alternative Library Literature* anthology includes an original report of a project in Santa Barbara, California, that I find not only immensely interesting, but also of great hope. To library administrators and gurus, who tend to be WASP-oriented and largely identify with middle- and upper-class society, people who don't use libraries are usually written off as not worth approaching. The rationale: "They don't use them, they don't tell us what they want, so why the hell bother with them? Let's stay with the monied, propertied clientele who look like us, who think like us, who run most everything that counts, and who we *know* want 75 copies of the latest blockbuster plus up-to-date, even if rather expensive, business and investment services." All right, what explodes that sort of narrow-minded attitude is the kind of thing that two Latino colleagues report in the study about Santa Barbara. That was how a whole population of nonlibrary users, Spanish-speaking, was activated to regard the library as a primary resource and a community focus: a source of information, a source of inspiration, a place to get together, everything we ordinarily assume a library ideally ought to be and what well-to-do, White, English-speaking people have always been using the library for. The report tells how they did it, and it took extra money, I'll admit. But more important than the money, I think, is the matter of the attitude, the desire to "go after" these people (in a good sense) and make them aware of what was potentially available in the library that would be useful to them. And, indeed, to ask *them* what they wanted from the library, which is almost heretical, because this hearkens back to the elitist notion that *we* know better than *they* what's good for them. We'll get the right books, we'll get the right services for them. The Santa Barbara experience shows that this won't wash anymore, and that the better kind of approach is what these writers call co-production, that is, community-library collaboration in supplying library services. It's a very inspiring report, with obvious implications for how best to service poor, unemployed, disabled, gay/lesbian, "counter-culture," and other ethnic communities: people who may not precisely look, think, or behave "just like us," but nonetheless deserve just as much attention and respect.

*Dwyer:* Given existing attitudes, to paraphrase Kris Kristofferson, is our profession "a walking contradiction, partly truth and partly fiction?"

*Berman:* In many respects it is, but always with honorable exceptions. I refuse to badmouth the whole profession. But I think that we, by and large, perpetuate too many mystifying and barrier-making practices, sometimes in the way we behave individually. Lawrence Ferlinghetti, commenting about both museum directors and library personnel, says that too often—here I'm paraphrasing slightly—they appear to be people who never go to the bathroom. In other words, people that you can't really approach because they're not quite human beings. They're on a pedestal, on a level above you, much like judges deliberately are, with the black robes and the high seat, producing a sort of intimidating atmosphere. So I think there are too many things we do that may cast us as distant, mystifying, unapproachable people and some practices we seem not to protest nearly enough in order to get them changed. In cataloging, as an example, abbreviations and slash marks and other kinds of "odd" punctuation persist, things that I'm convinced research will demonstrate — if anyone chooses to perform the damn research — most people don't understand, and yet we continually operate on the assumption that they either *do* understand or if they don't, they *should*. In short, we're members of a mystery cult. *We* know and it's enough that *we* know, and if *they* want to know, they're going to have to ask us, and if it bothers them too much, too bad.

*Dwyer:* Speaking of mystery cults, what about the Reagan administration's very successful efforts to restrict the flow of government information?

*Berman:* Perhaps for this interview it would be wasteful to talk about information policy at great length inasmuch as other people — like Zoia Horn, who's been jailed for civil disobedience, for standing up against government coercion — have done it far better and more eloquently than I ever could. Zoia, for example, does just that in a SIPAPU interview with Noel Peattie reprinted in the next *Alternative Library Literature*. Suffice it to say that the attack upon information, documented alike by ALA's Office for Intellectual Freedom and many authors and publishers, has been phenomenal. It involves excessive security classification of documents that clearly ought to be in the public domain. It involves scandalous cutbacks in producing and distributing important government documents, some of them medical. It involves precensorship of government employees themselves. It involves deliberate disinformation on the government's part, as for instance in the cases of Grenada and Nicaragua. It involves the exclusion of "dangerous" foreigners like Farley Mowat and the extraordinary effort to deport the U.S.-born writer, Margaret Randall, solely on account of her political views. It involves trashing films and pamphlets, like OSHA warnings to workers about occupational hazards, that don't fit the new "party line" and may adversely affect the national "business climate." It involves all these things. They've been well documented and the wonder is that more people seem not to be aware of this grand assault upon their own rights to information. This includes the press to a certain degree because I think they haven't complained loudly nor bitterly enough about what's happening to them, about how Reaganism is shrinking or polluting their own information sources. Also, I might toss in the increasing attempts to privatize information, to sell whole library services and databases. This information has been paid for by all of us through tax dollars and simply on that basis, if no other, we should have the right to access. Privatizing it means that somebody else benefits privately, commercially, from the very research, the very information that our tax dollars produced. The commercial interests who buy the database or service may then deny that very information or service to the public through elimination of "unprofitable" elements and even more seriously by pricing it too high for most of us, including a lot of libraries, to afford. Very often it was free or available at a nominal cost before privatizing, before this onslaught against government information, against its free access.

*Dwyer:* But then librarians themselves are sometimes known to precensor or self-censor.

*Berman:* They sure-as-hell do, and in a variety of ways.

*Dwyer:* Sex, censorship, and social change are hot topics these days. I know you consider sex and social change to be appropriate. What about censorship?

*Berman:* At one time earlier in my career, I would have described myself as a 100%-First-Amendment-intellectual-freedom-purist, as indeed many colleagues remain. I would now describe myself as certainly a civil libertarian, and always have been. I don't favor censorship, but I do believe that a good many issues of late, particularly dealing with pornography and also with stereotypical depictions of minority groups and attacks upon them in print and otherwise, can't any longer be dismissed with the simple purist argument that such depictions, that such treatments, are totally and automatically protected by the First Amendment. I think this may be the wrong place to get into specifics, but a great deal of argumentation, some of which I've contributed to, appears in past issues of the *Interracial Books for Children Bulletin*. The problem revolves around 14th versus 1st Amendment protections. The moral, social, and Constitutional aspects of these matters, particularly concerning how certain "speech" may gravely harm minorities and how pornography may injure women by inciting or predisposing towards sexism and violence, need a whole lot more discussion than we've accorded them. I think frankly that the other side — and there *is* a rational, temperate "other side" — has not been allowed its full say, notably in library and intellectual freedom circles. I don't think we've taken them seriously. And I've actually witnessed a "purist" — a librarian — talk herself right out of a meaningful public debate on antiporn civil rights laws due to her rigid, all-or-nothing position. Maybe this is the right place to further note, with continuing bitterness and disappointment, that the profession itself — through ALA — some years ago produced an ostensibly anticensorship film, *The Speaker,* that actually *promoted* racism, shamelessly and insensitively "using" and defaming Blacks to make its muddled point about "free speech."

*Dwyer:* One of the ideals of librarianship is that libraries should have balanced collections reflecting all points of view. This is a wonderful theory but is probably practiced more in the breach than in the observance. If we do achieve balanced collections, how can we promote positive social change like the elimination of racism and sexism?

*Berman:* Well, there are a number of ways. One way individually, personally, is being more of an activist on social issues within such structures as ALA's Social Responsibilities Round Table and its many task forces or within a group like Librarians for Nuclear Arms Control. Somewhat apart from the job, perhaps, but nonetheless related to it, librarians can participate in not only the obvious things like demonstrations, signing petitions, and sending letters to newspapers and legislators, but also do what we're more skilled at doing, like preparing bibliographies, mounting provocative, enlightening displays at meetings and fairs, conducting booktalks for neighborhood and special-interest groups, and writing reviews for the local and professional press, thus highlighting and publicizing material that represents lively, challenging, alternative viewpoints with the hope that some of this may then translate into actual social change, helping to make the world at once fairer, safer, and more fun. The other way, inside institutions and without violating intellectual freedom strictures, would be to actively participate in the programming and collection development processes, even though not officially designated as a collection developer or program librarian. For instance, there's no reason why somebody can't suggest that a program under library auspices might feature a Helen Caldicott film followed by a panel of community experts and activists discussing nuclear power and nuclear war. Why not recommend a staff training session that kicks off with the COSWL slide-tape show on women's library service and concludes with presentations by guests who describe local women's publications, bookstores and services? In our library, I'm not a material selector but I've always felt since entering librarianship that it's part of being a librarian to contribute at least suggestions to improve the library's collection in whatever areas I feel I have some expertise or special interest. So, as a result, not massively, but when it's appropriate, I submit recommendations for audiovisual and print items in the social change and alternative spheres to our material selection people, who are then free either to accept or reject them. They have, however, been very receptive, and I think this may well be true elsewhere when somebody tries to do the same thing. I almost religiously read alternative media, where there will surely be reviews of recent books, tapes, and films on the Sandinista regime in Nicaragua, on famine in the Third World and the multinationals' responsibility for much of it, on economic democracy and community empowerment and nuclear free zones and economic conversion and women's shelters and the Green Movement and animal rights. Reviews, too, of labor, gay, protest, and feminist songs on record labels like Redwood, Paredon, and Flying Fish. These kinds of things seldom if ever get reviewed in the standard journals that the collection development people consult and so they may warmly welcome the help that a Sandy Berman or a Jim Dwyer provides in order to make truly balanced and diverse a collection that otherwise would be molded by strictly mainstream concerns and only orthodox sources.

*Dwyer:* So even though we may not be material selectors, our selections are not immaterial. How is the vitality, the economic condition of the small and alternative presses these days?

*Berman:* Well, I can't claim to be an expert on alternative press economics, but my judgment — based upon just the Twin Cities area of Minnesota, if that's even moderately typical — is that the small, alternative press (nontraditional publishers dealing with experimental forms of literature, with new ideas, and with frankly radical, progressive, unusual lifestyles and politics) is indeed thriving. Frankly, I'm not prepared to say what audience it reaches, and I'd like to see some research done on that. But there's definitely a vital wealth of alternative activity, and not just limited to print. It's also in films, in independently produced video, and in alternative radio, community radio. We've got a splendid station called KFAI, "Fresh Air Radio," which is the only source in town where you can regularly hear Gay and Lesbian programming. They broadcast something like two and a half solid hours of reggae and all manner of not only classical but also folk and ethnic music. And not solely music, but also background cultural reports and news. "Fresh Air" has a very heavy commitment to Latin American programming. They've got at least two hours on Sunday where the news is presented bilingually from Latin America, reporting the latest developments and even including excerpts from the Sandinista news service, viewpoints and details seldom encountered in the big city dailies, network TV, and commercial radio stations.

*Dwyer:* Bringing this back home, one of the sources for alternatives and multiculturalism in libraries is to have the *Hennepin County List of Subject Headings.* The Library of Congress claims to follow the principle of specificity in *LC Subject Headings* but the Hennepin list seems much more specific, straightforward, and timely. Headings such as "Alcoholic professional workers," "Frozen yogurt," and "Product tampering" come to mind.

*Berman:* Yes, and a great many more come to mind if you examine our latest bimonthly *Bulletin* or simply scan our authority file, which comes out quarterly on fiche. Some time ago, we tried to earmark those forms where we deliberately either departed from the Library of Congress, making a substitution where we think it enhances findability, or, on the other hand, where it's the legitimate, self-preferred, fairer term from the standpoint of group or ethnic nomenclature. LC has followed the imperialist or, if you will, the white Western prejudice with respect to a peoples' names. Prototypically, for instance, the "Eskimos" we call "Inuit" at HCL and indicate in a "public note" that these are the people of such-and-such an area who are popularly but erroneously called "Eskimos." We do this same thing for a number of other peoples, not a great number, but—as examples—"Romanies" for "Gypsies," and also "Sami" for "Lapps," "Gay men" instead of LC's "Homosexuals, Male," and "Hansen's Disease patients" rather than the stigmatizing "Lepers."

*Dwyer:* But what about the criticism that these are not the headings that American library users will look under and you are therefore restricting access by using them?

*Berman:* That objection has been made frequently, and lately in letters from the Library of Congress itself. I'll admit right up front that there is a head-on collision here between two principles, both of which I ordinarily find holy. One is findability, being able to pop into the catalog and on a first search discover what it is you're looking for. That's one principle. The other one, however, which I invoke in this case and must assign superiority or dominance to, is the principle of equity or fairness. It's a head-on collision recognizing that people are more likely still to be looking first under "Eskimos" and then would have to be referred by a "see" reference to "Inuit." What I maintain is not only the equity principle, namely that it's fair, that it's right, but also that it's a mistake that we're correcting. Now, granted, it wasn't originally a *library* mistake. I'm not going to lay this burden on LC catalogers of fifty or sixty years ago. They were and still are, unfortunately, following what had been an established Western practice. But the point is that it *was* a mistake originally which has simply been perpetuated, so I view it — apart from the matter of equity — as a matter of correcting a mistake, of recti-fying an error, and in the process performing a kind of pedagogic function within the catalog, which is something salutary. To get kind of folksy about equity and fairness and legitimacy, it's as if someone insisted upon calling you Dick, even though you protested that your name was Jim. If someone still persistently called you Dick, wouldn't it be offensive? Wouldn't it be just plain inaccurate and wrong? I'm not suggesting that a lot of "Eskimos" have written us saying that, hey, we want this heading changed because we don't like it. But the point is that they've expressed their wishes in other forms and it's then relatively simple and — I'd insist — professionally mandated that we in-vestigate these claims and, once satisfied that we *have* made a mistake or are continuing a mistake, correct it. Hopefully, that would contribute to a greater sense of respect for other peoples, particularly smaller groups, folk peoples, who otherwise aren't in the limelight and can't afford heavy lobbying apparatus to get their way and to make their desires known. I think that we're big enough and smart enough and ultimately compassionate and sensitive enough that we can do these things without being clobbered first.

*Dwyer:* Besides providing access, you're promoting the radical idea that libraries are actually educational and cultural institutions.

*Berman:* Yes. How about that! Let me also say this. You also mentioned, in that survey alluded to earlier, that people found international issues to be a very low priority and perhaps on one plane, that's understandable. What's close to home is really what's more important. But since we're talking radical and unusual and off-beat and off-the-wall, I'd like to note that a strain in the major religions, though I don't claim to be an active religionist, and also a major Western literary and philosophical theme, represented by John Donne, for instance, in that famous passage, "For whom the bell tolls? It tolls for thee," is the idea that we're all, no matter where we happen by accident to live — whether it's Chico, California, Minneapolis, Minnesota, or Johan-nesburg, South Africa — connected to each other, responsible for one another. That there's a bond between us. This almost sounds mystical. I don't mean it to, but I do feel that something of the sort should exist, a bond of solidarity and mutual support between peoples so that we are not islands unto ourselves. And so I think that some international issues really do have practical library ramifications.

For instance, at this [1986] ALA conference, there's a resolution concerning Apartheid—which I helped draft—that will come before the SRRT Action Council and full ALA membership. It makes a number of points that tie in American library practice with the horror that has been the reality of life for most of South Africa's population for many, many years. For example, it deals with OCLC expanding its services to South Africa although the whole trend has been for American divestment in order to indicate displeasure with the Apartheid regime and to weaken it. That's one point. Another is that it's been discovered, and I'm embarrassed to say that I only learned this yesterday, that Forest Press, perhaps necessarily wanting to revise Dewey's South African history schedule, the 968s, went to South Africa for advice, which doesn't sound so bad. But they went to SAILIS, the reconstituted South African Library Association, which is still racially exclusive. SAILIS apparently appointed one or two people at a university in the Orange Free State, the bastion of Afrikaner racism and nationalism, to make recommendations for restructuring the schedule, which I understand a number of Africanists and particularly *Africans* have found to be ghastly. So that was another point made in the resolution.

Still one more is that we have an obligation here because we have a possible influence as a country and even as individuals owning stock or contributing to pension funds that in turn invest our money in Apartheid. South Africa isn't that remote and isn't that invulnerable, so we have the chance to impact on the situation there for the better, to influence the emergence of a more humane society. Divestment is one way. And ALA, to its credit, has done that. There are other ways, too. We can make more information about Apartheid available, not just the slick freebees that the South African Information Service readily sends out, but also material from sources that authentically represent Black African nationalist and liberationist viewpoints: materials, for instance, produced by the International Defense and Aid Fund, The Africa Fund, and the African National Congress of South Africa, which for the better part of the century has been the leading liberation movement.

*Dwyer:* In a small and less dramatic way, the Hennepin List itself is a tool for linguistic liberation, but there have been arguments raised about its practical applicability. What do you think of the argument that using alternative headings is impossible because of higher standardization and inadequate authority control and because understaffed cataloging departments don't have time to examine or enhance records from bibliographic utilities?

*Berman:* Two things can be said about that and I don't want either of them to seem either bombastic or unduly hard upon colleagues elsewhere. I know that the attitudinal problems can be surmounted, that a certain amount of local tinkering and tampering with subject headings and cross-referencing (which otherwise isn't likely to be done by *any*body) is possible if you're willing to do it. On the other hand, what would make life simpler for all of us, particularly those of us who "tamper" more rather than less, would be if descriptive and subject cataloging were rationalized, modernized, and humanized at the national level, which, practically speaking, means at the Library of Congress. If they would be more like us, frankly, cataloging more like we do at Hennepin County, I really believe — and there's no particular egotism nor malicious satisfaction involved in this — that the catalog product everywhere would be cheaper for everybody and also far more useful and functional. It would work better because people would be finding what they're looking for where they expect to find it, without foolish cross-references and possibly search-killing second lookups, and also without missing it altogether because some library couldn't afford or didn't think to make the cross-reference to the crazy LC form, which is very often the case. And *what* they find, the bibliographic record itself, would make more sense and prove more helpful because it wouldn't be littered with undecipherable hieroglyphics but *would* contain more notes and descriptive data to make it easier for users to decide whether the entry they've found is really for a work they *want*.

*Dwyer:* I've been told even by people who admire and use the list that they know more about Sandy Berman's ideas than they know about Sandy himself. You're a pretty busy fellow, a section head, a generator of subject headings, an activist, an author, an editor, and a one-man SDI service to a loose-knit network of librarians and others interested in language, human rights, alternative media, and the Incredible Hulk. How many hours do you log in a typical week?

*Berman:* I work an ordinary 8-hour day, a 40-hour week, but again it's hard for me to separate the personal from the professional and political. My wife and I celebrated our 18th wedding anniversary by having supper downtown in St. Paul and then attending a concert by the Klezmer Conservatory Band, which incidentally appears often on Garrison Keillor's "Prairie Home Companion." So we attended as part of our anniversary celebration. Well, what does that have to do with work? This is on a Saturday night; this has *nothing* to do with work. Except that on thinking about it afterwards, it struck me that the library probably didn't have much of anything by these performers, although it's vibrant, wonderful music and they're a terrific group. So I checked the catalog when I got back and it turned out that the only reference to them was by virtue of having been a cut on a "Prairie Home Companion" cassette. Because I'd earlier suggested a couple of discs by the Klezmorim, another group performing the same kind of music, we had a few Klezmer records. That's another story, by the way, because of the subject heading, since it's only about a year ago — after like literally pulling teeth — that LC recognized that there was something named "Klezmer music," although they've been playing the damn stuff and recording it for a helluva long time. So "Klezmer music" lately became a generally "kosher" subject heading though HCL innovated it first, naturally, but there were merely two or three entries under it in our own catalog, and only one for the Klezmer Conservatory Band. I suggested to our AV people that since this ensemble appears often on a widely enjoyed, locally-originating broadcast, and the music is good anyway, and they had three records out, maybe we should consider getting them. They *are* getting them, about five copies apiece. So we're going to have a delightful representation of Klezmer music in the library and while my enjoyment of that evening in St. Paul wasn't predicated on some kind of job outcome, nonetheless there *was* a job outcome. One thing sort of led to another. That happens a lot.

*Dwyer:* Recently, Kristin Ban Tepper, a library student, published a very interesting article about you in *Shmate*, "a journal of progressive Jewish thought." It was called, "What Makes Sandy Run?" What *does* make Sandy run?

*Berman:* A couple cups of coffee in the morning, walking half-a-mile around the corridors at work at about 11 a.m., and making sure I get in a nice little stroll outside at lunchtime. And I guess a certain degree of just plain compulsion and craziness because there's a lot of things I want to get done and I make myself do them.

*Dwyer:* It's important to note that you don't always criticize, but that you always have some sort of constructive solutions or alternatives.

*Berman:* Well, I'm glad you noticed that because it *has* been like an article of faith with me not simply to assail AACR2 or LC subject heading practice without being able to say that I was either prepared to do what I'm recommending that *they* do, or else that we've done it already. In most cases, we've done it already. We have proved it was possible and perhaps also that it was useful.

*Dwyer:* You seem to have a complex and changing relationship both with ALA and with the so-called Establishment Library Press. You're not a member of ALA, and don't always attend conferences, but you seem to be a speaker at conferences more frequently. ALA refused to publish *Prejudices and Antipathies,* yet RTSD presented you with the Margaret Mann Award in 1981. What's going on here?

*Berman:* I don't know. I can't figure it out myself.

*Dwyer:* If there were such a thing as a king of the library world and you were it, what would you do besides probably abolish the monarchy?

*Berman:* That's precisely it, because I haven't much patience with kings, gurus, popes or ayatollahs. My view of the optimum workplace situation — although where I work we certainly haven't reached it yet — is that there ought to be the greatest amount of egalitarian interaction and collaboration, to the point, if possible, even of consensus, rather than rigid hierarchical systems and top-down, "in-group" decision making.

*Dwyer:* You claim that you haven't really accomplished a great deal. I think maybe you're being a little too coy or a little too hard on yourself. Seriously, what important changes have you helped contribute to?

*Berman:* In truth, and without intending to be coy, I'm not altogether sure, except that anecdotal feedback and some other bits and pieces of evidence suggest that some definite improvements, especially in cataloging practices, might possibly have been inspired either by my critiques or by the kinds of models that we've developed at Hennepin County over many years. Perhaps also in a less tangible way, my writings, correspondence, "Care" packages, and talks have moved some people individually and the profession collectively toward a more humane, people-centered outlook and way of doing things. I hope so. But I can't prove it.

*Dwyer:* Have you ever felt kind of hopeless with what you are doing? Have you ever felt so frustrated that you even considered a different career?

*Berman:* Frustrated, yes. But never to the point of considering a different career, which—in all candor—may stem from an utter lack of imagination about something else to do and even a certain lack of self-confidence about any kind of substitute activity. I guess that what keeps me in librarianship, even though it has at times been extremely frustrating and even perilous, is a sort of compulsion to share, particularly ideas and information. That accounts for the kind of networking activity which I confess transcends just library colleagues and spills over into the local and even national community. On discovering a piece of solid information that I suspect would interest, say, a small press person or somebody in a particular movement group, or a "new word" collector, I simply find myself unable to suppress the instinct, the impulse, to get it to that person. So this compulsion results in a kind of proactive, selective dissemination of information, except some would claim that maybe it's not so selective.

*Dwyer:* You mentioned not just frustration, but even peril. Is that referring to the Ugandan experience or here in the U.S., too?

*Berman:* Well, Uganda was physically and otherwise dangerous, but I can't honestly say that was because of being a librarian or holding "subversive" political views. Part of it was being Jewish after Idi Amin had become violently anti-Semitic, thrown out the Israelis, and then made declarations, for instance, that Hitler didn't do the job well enough, that kind of very familiar tripe. So that was one element. His troops, which were barely disciplined, didn't much care for interracial couples, and that's what we were. Also at that time guerrillas invaded the country which further complicated the whole scene. It got Amin and his minions even more anxious than they would have been ordinarily. In general, what reigned was a totalitarian and increasingly racist mentality. A lot of people born there—all Asians—faced ultimate deportation and, in the meantime, suffered many sorts of brutalization. So the whole scene was really bad and literally dangerous and we were lucky to get out as quickly as we did. So that was one case. "Dangerous" is doubtless too strong a word to use in terms of subsequent career experience, but "hostility," definitely.

*Dwyer:* So what's next for Sandy Berman?

*Berman:* I probably should take something like a two or three week cruise through the West Indies. But the Great Midwestern Bookshow's coming up soon and I promised to sit a few hours at both the *Minnesota Reviews* and National Writers Union tables, and *Technicalities* will shortly want another "Consumer, Beware!" column. And any day the page proofs should arrive for indexing *Alternative Library Literature.* And I want to keep the pressure on the two RTSD committees now deliberating on AACR2 and subject cataloging reforms, and. . . .

# BERMANIANA: A SELECT BIBLIOGRAPHY

# SELECT CHRONOLOGICAL
# BIBLIOGRAPHY

- "Spanish Guinea: enclave empire," *Phylon,* v. 17 (Dec. 1956), p. 349–64.
  Comments/citations: Max Liniger-Goumaz, *Historical dictionary of Equatorial Guinea* (Scarecrow Press, 1979), p. 206.

- *Spanish Guinea: an annotated bibliography* (Catholic University of America Libraries, 1961), 2 v. (597 p.) Master's thesis.
  "A unique contribution to African Studies, and anyone doing research on Spanish Guinea will find it invaluable."—Helen F. Conover, comp., *Africa south of the Sahara: a selected, annotated list of writings* (Library of Congress, 1963), p. 319.

  "Monumental.... The only major bibliographical work produced by a non–Spanish author and devoted to Spanish Guinea. The service rendered to African Studies by the writer cannot be overestimated, since he has brought not merely a technical competence to his task but also a scientific impartiality—a quality often unknown to Iberian authors."—Rene Pelissier, "Spanish Africa: a bibliographical survey," *Africana newsletter,* v. 2, no. 2 (1964), p. 13.

  "By far the most exhaustive bibliography ever compiled on any Spanish possession is ... Berman's excellent ... work [which includes] a helpful introduction, a main and supplementary bibliography, glossary, chronology, directory of publishers, and index. Certainly the serious student of Spanish Africa cannot do without this indispensable aid."—William D. Jackson, "Survey of the literature available at UCLA on the Spanish territories in Africa," in California. University. Graduate Academy, 3d, Los Angeles, April 11–12, 1965, *Proceedings* (UCLA, 1966), p. 304.

  Further comments/citations: Peter Duignan, ed., *Guide to research and reference works on Sub-Saharan Africa* (Hoover Institution, Stanford University, 1972), p. 859; D.H. Varley, "Spanish-speaking Africa," in Conference on the Acquisition of Material from Africa, Birmingham University, 25 April 1969, *Reports and papers,* comp. by Valerie Bloomfield (Inter-Documentation, 1969), p. 73; Rene Pelissier, *Territorios españoles de Africa* (I.D.E.A., 1964), p. 91; *Africa South of the Sahara, 1973* (Europa Publications, 1973), p. 303; Max Liniger-Goumaz, *Historical dictionary of Equatorial Guinea* (Scarecrow Press, 1979), p. 177, 188.

- "Spanish Africa," in Helen Kitchen, ed., *Educated African* (Praeger, 1962), p. 302–14.
  Comments/citations: Pelissier, *Territorios españoles de Africa,* p. 91.

- Co-Editor, *Yin-yang.* nos. 1–2 (1966). Soldier-authored magazine, produced under auspices of Coleman and Taukkunen Barracks Special Services Libraries (Worms/Mannheim-Sandhofen, West Germany); copies archived at Dept. of Special Collections, UCLA Research Library.

- "Where it's at," *Library journal*, v. 93, no. 22 (Dec. 15, 1968), p. 4615–18. Reprinted, with some corrections and additions, in Eric Moon, ed., *Book selection and censorship in the sixties* (Bowker, 1969), p. 145–51.
  Comments/citations: Bill Katz, "Serials selection," in Walter C. Allen, ed., *Serial publications in large libraries* (Grad. School of Library Science, Univ. of Illinois, 1970), p. 22; Bill Katz, *Magazine selection: how to build a community-oriented collection* (Bowker, 1971), p. 117–18, 123; *Sipapu*, v. 1, no. 2 (July 1970), p. 5–6.

- "Dissident magazines," in Bill Katz, *Magazines for libraries* (Bowker, 1969), p. 104–14. Twenty-four annotations plus introduction.

- "Black Americana for African libraries," Zambia Library Association *Journal*, v. 1, no. 1 (June 1969), p. 15–19.

- "African magazines for American libraries," *Library journal*, v. 95, no. 7 (April 1, 1970), p. 1289–93. Subsequently updated and expanded in *LJ* "Magazines" column: Jan. 15, 1971, p. 177; Feb. 1, 1971, p. 457. Original text reprinted in Robert D.H. Sallery and others, eds., *Readings in development* (Canadian University Service Overseas, 1971), v. 3, p. 549–53. Also reprinted, with some revisions, in *Lotus: Afro-Asian writings*, no. 11 (Jan. 1972), p. 10–16.
  Comments/citations: *Current bibliography on African affairs*, New ser., v. 3, no. 7 (July 1970), p. 30; Grant T. Skelley, "Bibliography: Africa," in Bill Katz, *Magazines for libraries*, 2d ed. (Bowker, 1972), p. 768; *Sipapu*, v. 1, no. 2 (July 1970), p. 4–5.

- Editor, *Periodicals currently received at the University of Zambia Library: April 1970* (Univ. of Zambia Library, 1970). 159 p.

- "Subject: Zambia; a selection of recent items in periodicals received at the University Library," Zambia Library Association *Journal*, v. 2, no. 4 (Dec. 1970), p. 9–15.

- "Let it all hang out; a think-piece for Luddite librarians," *Library journal*, v. 96, no. 12 (June 15, 1971), p. 2054–58.
  Reprints: Bill Katz, ed. *Library lit. 2: the best of 1971* (Scarecrow Press, 1972), p. 392–404; Patricia Glass Schuman, comp., *Social responsibilities and libraries: a Library journal/School library journal selection* (Bowker, 1976), p. 341–49.
  Comments/citations: "Letters," *Library journal*, Sept. 1, 1971, p. 2561–62, Feb. 15, 1972, p. 616, March 15, 1972, p. 951; John Tebbel, "The role of technology in the future of libraries," in *The metropolitan library* (MIT Press, 1972), p. 257; Sara F. Fine, "Technological innovation, diffusion and resistance: an historical perspective," *Journal of library administration*, v. 7, no. 1 (Spring 1986), p. 88, 106.

- Editor, Makerere Institute of Social Research Library *Accessions list/bulletin* (Kampala). Monthly. July 1971–Sept. 1972.
  February 1972 editorial reprinted in March/April 1974 *CALL* (v. 3, no. 2), p. 14, as "The indexing of Black African library literature."
  Comments/citations: *American libraries*, v. 3, no. 8 (Sept. 1972), p. 923; *Sipapu*, v. 3, no. 1 (Jan. 1973), p. 5; Sheila Goldstein, comp., "Preliminary bibliography on Africana cataloging," *Africana libraries newsletter*, no. 6 (June 1976), p. 18.

- Compiler, *Periodicals at the Makerere Institute of Social Research Library: September 1971* (Kampala). 22 p.

- *Prejudices and antipathies; a tract on the LC subject heads concerning people* (Scarecrow Press, 1971). 249 p. Excerpts, titled "Children, 'idiots,' the 'underground,' and others," published in *School library journal*, Dec. 1971, p. 36–41.
  Reviews: Seymour Lubetsky, *Library journal*, Feb. 15, 1972, p. 658–59 [rejoinder:

"Counter cataloging," May 1, 1972, p. 1640-42]; Charles Rudd, *Freethinker*, March 4, 1972, p. 79; Jonathan S. Tyron, *Newsletter on intellectual freedom*, July 1972, p. 112 [rejoinder: May 1973, p. 58]; Arthur W. Uloth, *Freedom*, April 29, 1972, p. 2; Nancy Musser, *Synergy*, Summer 1972, p. 37; Noel Peattie, *Sipapu*, July 1972, p. 6-10; Joseph Z. Nitecki, *Library quarterly*, July 1972, p. 355-57; Kyung W. Son, *Canadian library journal*, Sept./Oct. 1972, p. 427; Sarwar A. Siddigui, *Pakistan library bulletin*, Sept./Dec. 1972, p. 74-5; *Interracial books for children*, Winter 1972/73, p. 10; Hazel Waters, *Race today*, April 1973, p. 120; H.A. Kanitkar, *New community*, Autumn 1973, p. 438-39; Kwame E. Avafia, *Nigerian libraries*, v. 9, no. 3 (1973), p. 205-06; J.R. Moore, *Library resources & technical services*, Winter 1974, p. 73-6.

Comments/citations: *ALA/SRRT newsletter*, Nov. 1971, p. 15; Joan K. Marshall, "LC labeling: an indictment," in Celeste West and Elizabeth Katz, eds., *Revolting librarians* (Booklegger Press, 1972), p. 45-9; Doris Cruger Dale, "Library schools in Africa: a preliminary survey," *Illinois libraries*, Sept. 1972, p. 485-86; Gail Von Hahmann, *Report on Fall 1971 visit to eight African countries* (Research Liaison Committee, African Studies Assn., 1972), p. 17; *Current bibliography on African affairs*, New ser., v. 5, no. 2 (March 1972), p. 220; Marvin H. Scilken, "Relevant subject headings," *Unabashed librarian*, Nov. 1971, p. 11; "Race and schools and related topics: bibliography," *Integrated education*, May/June 1972, p. 80; *LC information bulletin*, Dec. 30, 1971, p. 750, March 3, 1972, p. 94; San Francisco Bay Area SRRT, *Racism: readings for the front of the bus* (Nov. 1972), p. 1; Mary McKenney, "Librarianship as a subversive activity," *Synergy*, no. 39 (Nov. 24, 1972), p. 1; Joan K. Marshall, "Viewpoint: prejudice through Library of Congress subject headings," *Newsletter on intellectual freedom*, Nov. 1971, p. 126-27; S.A.H. Abidi, *Management of libraries: classification and cataloging* (Dar es Salaam: Seminar on Library Management, 1972), p. 9, 12; Mildred Dickeman, "Racism in the library: a model from the public schools," *School library journal*, Feb. 1973, p. 613-14; various course reading lists and bibliographies (e.g., Library Science 206, Louisiana State Univ., 1972; LS 630, "Advanced cataloging and classification," Western Michigan Univ., 1973); Helen R. Wheeler, *Womanhood media* (Scarecrow Press, 1972), p. 85; Samuel Goldstein, *CALL*, Nov./Dec. 1973, p. 2; "Poverty of thinking," *Race today*, Oct./Nov. 1973, p. 302 (part of special feature on "Books, libraries and racism"); Elizabeth Dickinson, "A word game," *Emergency librarian*, Feb. 1974, p. 4-7; Joan K. Marshall, "A new look at organizing materials in academic libraries," in E.J. Josey, ed., *New dimensions for academic library service* (Scarecrow Press, 1975), p. 139; Dorothy Kanwischer, "Subject headings trauma," *Wilson library bulletin*, May 1975, p. 654; Bill Katz, *Magazines for libraries* (2d ed. supplement; Bowker, 1974), p. ix, 171; Ian C.S. Britain, "Classification and culture," *Australian academic & research libraries*, March 1975, p. 34-5, 43; *African book publishing record*, April 1975, p. 133; Jessica L. Harris, "Document description and representation," in *Annual review of information science and technology*, v. 9 (1974), p. 105, 111; "Cataloging notes," *Africana libraries newsletter*, Nov. 1975, p. 7; Maurice J. Freedman, "Processing for the people," *Library journal*, Jan. 1, 1976, p. 197; Doris H. Clack, *Black literature resources: analysis and organization* (M. Dekker, 1975), p. 195; Freedman, "Cataloging systems: 1973 applications status," in Susan K. Martin and Brett Butler, eds., *Library automation: the state of the art II* (A.L.A., 1975), p. 80; Arlene Taylor Dowell, *Cataloging with copy: a decision-maker's handbook* (Libraries Unlimited, 1976), p. 128, 285; Sheila Goldstein, comp., "Preliminary bibliography on Africana cataloging," *Africana libraries newsletter*, June 1976, p. 18; Michael Gorman, *RQ*, v. 17, no. 3 (Spring 1978), p. 265; Lois Mai Chan, "The principle of uniform heading in Library of Congress subject headings," *Library resources & technical services*, v. 22, no. 2 (Spring 1978), p. 129, 136; Doris Hargrett Clack, "The adequacy of Library of Congress subject headings for Black literature resources," *ibid.*, p. 137-38, 143; Pamela Walker, "A rationale for the use of split files for subject headings," *ibid.*, p. 156; William J. Pease, "Black subjects, White subjectivity," *California librarian*, v. 34, no. 2 (April 1978), p. 40-41, 45; Mildred Dickeman, "Mostly for Whites: a course on white racism," in Miriam Wolf-Wasserman and Linda Hutchinson, eds., *Teaching human dignity: social change lessons for every teacher* (Minneapolis: Education Exploration Center, 1978), p. 57; Charlie Lumkins, "FASTCAT," *PLAFSEP*, no. 6 (Spring 1979), p. 4 ("Examples of subject heading changes ... I have made are found in ... *Prejudices and antipathies*"); Jessica L. Milstead Harris and Doris H. Clack, "Treatment of people and peoples in subject analysis," *Library resources & technical services*, v. 23, no. 4 (Fall 1979), p. 375+ ; Bohdan S. Wynar, *Introduction to cataloging and classification* (6th ed.; Littleton, CO: Libraries Unlimited, 1980), p. 500, 517, 641; Emmett A. Davis and Catherine M. Davis, *Mainstreaming library service for disabled people* (Scarecrow Press, 1980), p. 101, 111, 123, 137, 140; Michael Gorman, "AACR2: main themes," in *The making of a code: the issues underlying AACR2* (Chicago: A.L.A., 1980), p. 50; Michael Gorman, "How the machine may yet save LCSH," *American libraries*, Oct. 1980, p. 557; Donnarae Mac-Cann, "On equal terms: the classics," *SSRT newsletter*, #57 (Sept. 1980), p. 2; Monica A. Greaves, "Cataloging and classification: the Nigerian scene," in Mohammed M. Aman, ed., *Cataloging and classification of non-Western material* (Oryx Press, 1980), p. 25, 29; *Report of the Racism and Sexism in Subject Analysis Subcommittee to the RTSD/CCS Subject Analysis Committee, Midwinter 1980* (3d revision, June 1980), p. 13, Appendix 2, p. 2-3, 6, 9, Appendix 5, p. 1; Edward T. O'Neill and Rao Aluri, "Library of Congress subject heading patterns in OCLC monographic records," *Library resources & technical services*, Jan./March 1981, p. 79; Adolphe O. Amadi, *African libraries: Western tradition and colonial brainwashing* (1981), p. 183, 198, 247; Leith Peterson, "Ojibway-Cree Resource Centre classification conversion program," *Ontario library review*, v. 65, no. 1 (March 1981), p. 49; William A. Katz, *Introduction to reference work* (3d ed.; McGraw-Hill, 1978), v. 2, p. 100; A.C. Foskett, *Subject approach to information*, 3d ed. (Clive Bingley/Linnet Books, 1977), p. 101; Marty Bloomberg and G. Edward Evans, "Bibliography—cataloging," in their *Introduction to technical services for library technicians* (4th ed.; Libraries Unlimited, 1981), p. 350; Gail J. Junion, "Guide to reference tools for cataloging Africana," *Library resources & technical services*, v. 26, no. 2 (April/June 1982), p. 121; Monika Kirtland and Pauline Cochrane, "Critical views of *LCSH*—Library of Congress subject headings: a bibliographic and bibliometric essay," *Cataloging & classification quarterly*, v. 1, nos. 2/3 (1982), p. 87-8; William Mischo, "Library of Congress subject headings: a review of the problems and prospects for improved subject access," *ibid.*, p. 122; Robert P. Holley and Robert E. Killheffer, "Is there an answer to the subject access crisis?," *ibid.*, p. 133; John C. Swan, "Ethics at the reference desk: comfortable theories and tricky practices," *Reference librarian*, no. 4 (Summer 1982), p. 103, 115; S.I.A. Kotei, *Trends in the classification and cataloging of materials relating to Africa* (paper presented at SCOLMA Conference on Progress in African Bibliography, London, March 1977), p. 27; Arthur Curley and Jana Varlejs, *Akers' simple library cataloging* (Scarecrow Press, 1984), p. 141; Pauline A. Cochrane, *Improving LCSH for use in online catalogs* (Libraries Unlimited, 1986), p. v; William E. Studwell, "Why not an 'AACR' for subject headings?," *Cataloging & classification quarterly*, v. 6, no. 1 (Fall 1985), p. 8. Multi-part "Supplement" published in *Ugandan libraries:* Fall 1972, p. 21-6; March 1973, p. 18-23.

Comments/citations: *Sipapu*, Jan. 1973, p. 1.

• Compiler, *Subject headings employed at the Makerere Institute of Social Research Library; a select list: February 1972* (Kampala, Uganda: MISR Library, 1972). 56 p. Expanded, 102-page, photo-offset edition issued by Makerere University Library, May 1972, as no. 11 in its "Publications" series.

Comments/citations: *American libraries*, Sept. 1972, p. 923; *African studies newsletter*,

Sept./Oct. 1972, p. 63; *Africana library journal,* Summer 1972, p. 35; *Library materials on Africa,* July 1972, p. 78; *UNESCO bulletin for libraries,* March/April 1973, p. 112; H.M. Zell, "Scope and arrangement," in *African books in print* (Mansell, 1975), pt. 1, p. xvi-xvii; Sheila Goldstein, comp., "Preliminary bibliography on Africana cataloging," *Africana libraries newsletter,* June 1976, p. 18; S.I.A. Kotei, *Trends in the classification and cataloging of materials relating to Africa* (paper presented at SCOLMA Conference on Progress in African Bibliography, London, March 1977), p. 29.

- Compiler, *African liberation movements; a roster of material at the Makerere Institute of Social Research Library: April 1972* (MISR Library, 1972). 14 p. Reprinted, with some revisions, as "African liberation movements: a preliminary bibliography," *Ufahamu,* v. 3, no. 1 (Spring 1972), p. 107-28.
  Comments/citations: *Library materials on Africa,* July 1972, p. 78; *Radical Africana,* Oct. 1972, p. 12, 25; F.A. Kornegay, Jr., "Bibliographic memorial to Amilcar Cabral: selected survey of resources on the struggle in Guinea-Bissau," *Ufahamu,* v. 3, no. 3 (Winter 1973), p. 154.

- Compiler, *Women/sexism/the Feminist Movement; a roster of material at the Makerere Institute of Social Research Library: April 1972* (MISR Library, 1972). 12 p.
  Comments/citations: *News sheet; notes from the* [NOW] *Committee To Promote Women's Studies,* April 1974, p. 4.

- Compiler, *Workers' control/self-management/co-determination; a roster of material at the Makerere Institute of Social Research Library: April 1972* (MISR Library, 1972). 6 p.

- Compiler, *African liberation movements and support groups: a directory* (MISR Library, 1972). 8 p. Reprinted, with some corrections and additions, as "Directory: African liberation movements and support groups," *Ufahamu,* v. 3, no. 2 (Fall 1972), p. 170-88.
  Comments/citations: Alfred Kagan, *African National Congress of South Africa: a bibliography* (NY: United Nations Centre Against Apartheid, 1982), p. 2; *Current bibliography on African affairs,* New ser., Sept./Nov. 1972, p. 594; *Radical Africana,* Oct. 1972, p. 25; *Current bibliography on African affairs,* Winter 1973, p. 96.

- "Libraries to the people!," in Celeste West and Elizabeth Katz, eds., *Revolting librarians* (Booklegger Press, 1972), p. 51-7. Updated reprint of article originally published in the Los Angeles *Free press,* March 1971.

- Consultant/contributor to Bill Katz, *Magazines for libraries,* 2d ed. (Bowker, 1972).

- "Uganda: speak in whispers, if at all," *Newsletter on intellectual freedom,* v. 22, no. 2 (March 1973), p. 27 + .
  Comments/citations: *Geneva-Africa,* v. 12, no. 1 (1973), p. 141-42.

- Editor, Hennepin County Library *Cataloging bulletin,* no. 1 (May 1973)-40 (May/June 1979). Bi-monthly.
  Reviews: Samuel Goldstein, *CALL,* Nov./Dec. 1973, p. 2 (reprinted in April 1974 *Emergency librarian,* p. 22-4); *MSRRT newsletter,* Jan./Feb. 1974, p. 3; Bill Katz, *Magazines for libraries,* 2d ed. supplement (Bowker, 1974), p. 171; Joan K. Marshall, *Booklegger magazine,* Nov./Dec. 1975, p. 24; James P. Danky/Michael Fox, *Wilson library bulletin,* May 1977, p. 765; Val Morehouse, *Booklist,* v. 74, no. 3 (Oct. 1, 1977), p. 271; Sydney Pierce, in *Magazines for libraries* (3d ed.; Bowker, 1978), p. 125.
  Index review: Allison Mook Sleeman, *Serials review,* v. 4, no. 4 (Oct./Dec. 1978), p. 67-8.
  Comments/citations: *Young adult alternative newsletter,* March 15, 1974, p. 9; *CALL,*

Sept./Oct. 1973, p. 2, 43; *Emergency librarian*, April 1974, p. 33; *American libraries*, May 1974, p. 264; *News sheet*, Dec. 1974, p. 2; *Emergency librarian*, Dec. 1974, p. 3; *SELCO scoop* (Rochester, Minnesota: SouthEastern Libraries Cooperation), Feb. 1975, p. 2; *Media report to women*, May 1, 1975, p. 10; Dorothy Kanwischer, "Subject headings trauma," *Wilson library bulletin*, May 1975, p. 654; Sarah Slavin Schramm, comp., *The raw materials of women's history: a bibliography*, issued as supplem. to *News sheet*, no. 8 (June 1975), p. 1; Steve Wolf, "Catalogers in revolt against LC's racist, sexist headings," *Interracial books for children bulletin*, v. 6, nos. 3/4 (1975), p. 3; Kirsten Grimstad/Susan Rennie, eds., *New woman's survival sourcebook* (Knopf, 1975), p. 159; Gail Whitney, "Update on little library and library-related serials," *American libraries*, Nov. 1975, p. 613; *RAIN*, Nov. 1975, p. 7; Carol Starr, "Reading to keep current: the whole Young Adult Librarian's professional serials selections," *Young adult alternative newsletter*, Nov. 15, 1975, p. 1, 3; Helen R. Wheeler, "Movements periodicals," in her *Womanhood media supplement* (Scarecrow Press, 1975), p. 135; *ALA/SRRT newsletter*, no. 37 (Jan. 1976), p. 3; Maurice J. Freedman, "Processing for the people," *Library journal*, Jan. 1, 1976, p. 193; "The library free press," *Booklegger magazine*, Feb. 1976, p. 25; *Resources*, Jan. 1, 1976, p. 8; Freedman, "Cataloging systems: 1973 applications status," in *Library automation: the state of the art II* (A.L.A., 1975), p. 82; E.J. Josey, "Social responsibilities," *ALA yearbook 1976*, p. 322-23; Lois Mai Chan, "Year's work in cataloging and classification: 1975," *Library resources & technical services*, Summer 1976, p. 218; Haverhill (Mass.) Public Library Technical Services Dept., *Staff manual* (1976), p. 4, 11, 38; *Sipapu*, July 1976, p. 16-17; *International directory of little magazines and small presses*, 1976/77 (12th ed.), p. 114; Phyllis Yaffe, "A free press in our lifetime," *Emergency librarian*, Sept./Oct. 1976, p. 27; *Wilson library bulletin*, March 1977, p. 556; *Sources*, v. 1, no. 1 (Winter 1977), p. 60; *Sunspark guide to alternative periodicals*, 1st supplement (May 1977), p. 61; *Newsletter on intellectual freedom*, May 1977, p. 70; Barbara M. Westby, ed., *Sears list of subject headings*, 11th ed. (Wilson, 1977), p. viii, xxxiv; *Music cataloging bulletin*, v. 8, no. 10 (Oct. 1977), p. 5-6; *LJ/SLJ hotline*, v. 7, no. 3 (Jan. 23, 1978), p. 4; Fred Lerner, "A classified vertical file," *Unabashed librarian*, no. 26 (1978), p. 3; Susan J. Hall, "What do textbooks teach our children about Africa?," *Interracial books for children bulletin*, v. 9, no. 3 (1978), p. 7; Valerie Wheat, "The library free press," in Celeste West and Valerie Wheat, *The passionate perils of publishing* (Booklegger Press, 1978), p. 70; Jewish Librarians Caucus *Newsletter*, v. 3, no. 2 (Spring 1978), p. 8-9; "New subject cataloging code proposed for school and public libraries," *LJ/SLJ hotline*, v. 8, no. 12 (March 26, 1979), p. 2; *PLAFSEP*, no. 6 (Spring 1979), p. 2; Emmett A. Davis, comp., *Mediagraphy on mainstreaming library service to disabled persons* (OPLIC, 1979), p. 6; Monika Kirtland and Pauline Cochrane, "Critical views of *LCSH*—Library of Congress subject headings: a bibliographic and bibliometric essay," *Cataloging & classification quarterly*, v. 1, nos. 2/3 (1982), p. 87-8; S.I.A. Kotei, *Trends in the classification and cataloging of materials relating to Africa* (paper presented at SCOLMA Conference on Progress in African Bibliography, London, March 1977), p. 28; Elliott Shore, "Collecting the alternative press," in *LJ special report* no. 11 (N.Y.: Bowker, 1979), p. 32, and "The alternative press and libraries," *Collection building*, v. 1, no. 3 (1979), p. 15, 17; Marilyn H. Jones, "Year's work in cataloging and classification: 1978," *Library resources and technical services*, v. 23, no. 3 (Summer 1979), p. 246-47, 250, 273, 276-77, 287-88; Margaret A. Rohdy, *Serials review*, v. 5, no. 3 (July/Sept. 1979), p. 25; Jean Weihs, with Shirley Lewis and Janet Macdonald, *Nonbook materials: the organization of integrated collections*. 2d ed. (Canadian Library Assn., 1979), p. 8, 131-32; *PLAFSEP*, no. 9 (Winter 1979/80), p. 6, 8; *Unabashed librarian*, no. 32 (1979), p. 4; Bohdan S. Wynar, *Introduction to cataloging and classification* (6th ed.; Littleton, CO: Libraries Unlimited, 1980), p. 500, 517, 520, 533, 631; Emmett A. Davis and Catherine M. Davis, *Mainstreaming library service for disabled people* (Scarecrow Press,

1980), p. 105–6; Constance Rinehart, "Year's work in descriptive cataloging: 1979," *Library resources & technical services*, v. 24, no. 3 (Summer 1980), p. 231; Doris Hargrett Clack, "Year's work in subject analysis: 1979," *Library resources & technical services*, v. 24, no. 3 (Summer 1980), p. 243; Shirley Miller, *The vertical file and its satellites* (2d ed.; Littleton, CO: Libraries Unlimited, 1979), p. 68, 227; Bella Hass Weinberg, "Hebraica cataloging and classification," in Mohammed M. Aman, ed., *Cataloging and classification of non-Western material: concerns, issues and practices* (Oryx Press, 1980), p. 356.

Winner, 1976 H.W. Wilson Library Periodical Award.

Reprinted articles, reviews, etc.: *Library journal*, Sept. 1, 1974, p. 2033–35; *Jewish Librarians Caucus newsletter*, March 1976, p. 4–6, July 1976, p. 6, April 1977, p. 14–17; *Law cataloger*, May 1976, p. 4–5, Jan. 1977, p. 8–9; *Interracial books for children bulletin*, v. 6, nos. 3/4 (1975), p. 16; *Unabashed librarian*, no. 19 (Spring 1976), p. 16; *CALL*, July/ Aug. 1976, p. 12–13; Haverhill (Mass.) Public Library, Technical Services Dept., *Staff manual* (1977), p. 7+; *Jewish Librarians Caucus newsletter*, v. 3, no. 1 (Winter 1978), p. 4; Bill Katz, ed., *Library lit. 7—The best of 1976* (Scarecrow Press, 1977), p. 138–41 (Doris Garton's "Card catalogue made specific," HCLCB #21); *Library lit. 9—the best of 1978* (Scarecrow Press, 1979), p. 138–53 (Maurice Freedman's "Some thoughts on public libraries and the national bibliographic network," HCLCB #28).

- Editor, *ALA/SRRT newsletter*, no. 28 (Nov. 1973)-35 (May 1975). Bi-monthly.

   Reviews: Samuel Goldstein, *CALL*, Mar./April 1974, p. 11–12; Bill Katz, *Library journal*, Nov. 15, 1974, p. 2951.

   Comments/citations: *Emergency librarian*, Feb. 1974, p. 19, South Bay SRRT *Newsletter*, Jan. 1974, p. 2; *Interracial books for children*, v. 5, no. 4 (1974), p. 5; *Booklegger magazine*, July/Aug. 1974, p. 46.

- "Cataloging philosophy: a prose-poem delivered at the HCL General Staff Meeting, 2-21-74," HCL *Cataloging bulletin*, nos. 6/7 (April 5, 1974), p. 9–13. Reprinted as "Cataloging philosophy: a prose poem," with illustrations by I. Jansons and editorial comment by John N. Berry, in *Library journal*, v. 99, no. 15 (Sept. 1, 1974), p. 2017, 2033–35. "Prose poem" alone republished in Bill Katz/Robert Burgess, eds., *Library lit. 5—the best of 1974* (Scarecrow Press, 1975), p. 147–52.

   Comments/citations: Marty Bloomberg and G. Edward Evans, "Bibliography— Cataloging," in their *Introduction to technical services for library technicians* (4th ed.; Libraries Unlimited, 1981), p. 350; "Letters," *Library journal*: Oct. 15, 1974, 2558–59, Nov. 1, 1974, p. 2783, Nov. 15, 1974, p. 2918, Dec. 1, 1974, p. 3074, Dec. 15, 1974, p. 3156, Jan. 1, 1975, p. 4, Jan. 15, 1975, p. 75–6, April 15, 1975, p. 703; Arlene Taylor Dowell, *Cataloging with copy* (Libraries Unlimited, 1976), p. 128, 285; William J. Pease, "Black subjects, White subjectivity," *California librarian*, v. 34, no. 2 (April 1978), p. 45.

- Consultant/contributor to Bill Katz, *Magazines for libraries*, 2d ed. supplement (Bowker, 1975).

- Compiler, "Index," in E.J. Josey, ed., *New dimensions for academic library service* (Scarecrow Press, 1975), p. 337–49.

   Comments/citations: Jovian Lang, *College & research libraries*, Sept. 1975, p. 427.

- "Rules for cataloging audio-visual materials at Hennepin County Library," in Deirdre Boyle, ed., *Expanding media* (Oryx Press, 1977), p. 265–72. Reprinted from *Unabashed librarian*, Spring 1973, p. 6–8.

- "CIP, subjects, and little presses," *COSMEP newsletter*, v. 7, no. 10 (July 1976),

p. 8. Reprinted as "Look before you leap: LC's C.I.P.," *Booklegger magazine,* v. 3, no. 15 (Summer 1976), p. 10–11.

- Compiler, *Alternative library publications* (Task Force on Alternative Library Publications, Nov. 1976; rev. ed., Jan. 1977). 4 p. Reprinted as "Alternative library periodicals," *CALL,* v. 5, no. 6 (Nov./Dec. 1976), p. 5–6.

- "Cataloging alternative media: part 1," *Collectors' Network news,* v. 1, no. 1 (Jan./Feb. 1977), p. 7–8.

- "Cataloging alternative media: part 2," *Collectors' Network news,* v. 1, no. 2 (March/April 1977), p. 4–6.

- Compiler, "Subject index," *Sources: a guide to print and nonprint materials available from organizations, industry, government agencies, and specialized publishers* (Gaylord Professional Publications), v. 1, no. 1 (Winter 1977), p. 173–78; v. 1, no. 2 (Spring 1977), p. 199–212; v. 1, no. 3 (Fall 1977), p. 177–98; v. 2, no. 1 (1978), p. 195–208; v. 2, no. 2 (1978), p. 168–87; v. 2, no. 3 (1979), p. 185–210; v. 3, no. 1 (1980), p. 175–89; v. 3, no. 2 (1980), p. 177–99; v. 3, no. 3 (1980), p. 155–85; v. 4, no. 1 (1981), p. 195–210; v. 4, no. 2 (1981), p. 173–99; v. 4, no. 3 (1981), p. 179–216; v. 5, no. 1 (1982), p. 195–212; v. 5, no. 2 (1982), p. 175–205; v. 5, no. 3 (1982), p. 165–206.

- "Nitty-gritty subject heads: a selection of people-helping descriptors LC hasn't got around to yet and a nifty idea to expand the usefulness of your catalog by reference to outside information sources," *Unabashed librarian,* no. 22 (1977), p. 8.
  Comments/citations: Monika Kirtland and Pauline Cochrane, "Critical views of *LCSH*— Library of Congress subject headings: a bibliographic and bibliometric essay," *Cataloging & classification quarterly,* v. 1, nos. 2/3 (1982), p. 87.

- "Catalogue of horrors," *Emergency librarian,* v. 4, no. 4 (March/April 1977), p. 6–10.
  Comments/citations: William A. Katz, *Introduction to reference work* (3d ed.; N.Y.: McGraw-Hill, 1978), v. 2, p. 100.

- Compiler, "Index," in E.J. Josey and Kenneth E. Peeples, eds., *Opportunities for minorities in librarianship* (Scarecrow Press, 1977), p. 191–201.

- "Cataloging shtik," *Library journal,* v. 102, no. 11 (June 1, 1977), p. 1251–53.
  Comments/citations: "Letters," *Library journal:* Sept. 1, 1977, p. 1693–94, Oct. 1, 1977, p. 1975; Michael Gorman and Jami Hotsinpiller, "ISBD: aid or barrier to understanding?," *College & research libraries,* v. 40, no. 6 (Nov. 1979), p. 519, 521; William Mischo, "Library of Congress subject headings: a review of the problems and prospects for improved subject access," *Cataloging & classification quarterly,* v. 1, nos. 2/3 (1982), p. 122; Robert P. Holley and Robert E. Killheffer, "Is there an answer to the subject access crisis?," *ibid.,* p. 133.

- "'The Speaker': not recommended," *Interracial books for children bulletin,* nos. 4/5 (1977), p. 19–20.
  Reprint: Bill Katz, ed., *Library lit. 8—the best of 1977* (Scarecrow Press, 1978), p. 274–76.

- Consultant/contributor to Joan K. Marshall, *On equal terms: a thesaurus for non-sexist indexing and cataloging* (Neal-Schuman, 1977).

- Compiler, *Kids' stuff: a grabbag of subject headings for (mostly) children's media* (Hennepin County Library, Oct. 1977). 6-panel folded bookmark.

- Compiler, "Index," in E.J. Josey and Ann Allen Shockley, eds., *Handbook of Black librarianship* (Libraries Unlimited, 1977), p. 367-92.

- Compiler, "Kids' stuff: a grabbag of Hennepin County (MN) Library subject headings for (mostly) children's media," *Unabashed librarian*, no. 25 (1977), p. 6-7.

- Compiler, "Alternative library lit.: publications of the 'small press' movement in librarianship," *Library journal*, v. 103, no. 1 (Jan. 1, 1978), p. 23-5.
  Updated reprint: Bill Katz, ed., *Library lit. 9 — the best of 1978* (Scarecrow Press, 1979), p. 406-15.
  Comments/citations: Elliot Shore, "Collecting the alternative press," in *LJ special report* no. 11 (N.Y.: Bowker, 1979), p. 32, and "The alternative press and libraries," *Collection building*, v. 1, no. 3 (1979), p. 17; Patricia J. Case, "Antidote to the homogenized library," *New pages*, no. 6 (Spring 1983), p. 7.

- Compiler, *Hey, consumer! A selection of consumer-related subject headings in the Hennepin County Library materials catalog.* (Hennepin County Library, Dec. 1977). 6-panel folded bookmark.
  Reprint: "A selection of consumer-related subject headings in the Hennepin County Library materials catalog," *Unabashed librarian*, no. 30 (1979), p. 13.
  Comments/citations (U*L reprint): Doris Hargrett Clack, "Year's work in subject analysis: 1979," *Library resources & technical services*, v. 24, no. 3 (Summer 1980), p. 240, 245.

- "ALA Publishing as censor: a bill of particulars," *CALL (Current awareness — library literature)*, v. 7, no. 1 (Jan./Feb. 1978), p. 4-5.
  Reprint: Bill Katz, ed., *Library lit. 9 — the best of 1978* (Scarecrow Press, 1979), p. 402-05.

- "Stop playing hide-and-seek with ethnic materials," *Wilson library bulletin*, v. 52, no. 9 (May 1978), p. 691, 719. Original, unedited version published in *HCL cataloging bulletin*, no. 35 (July/Aug. 1978) as "Ethnic access: new approaches in cataloging," p. 1-7.
  Comments/citations: Hans H. Wellisch, "Bibliographic access to multilingual collections," *Library trends*, v. 29, no. 2 (Fall 1980), p. 223, 243.

- "Gay access: new approaches in cataloging," Gay Teachers Association *Newsletter*, v. 1, no. 6 (June 1978), p. 1-2.
  Updated reprints: *Gay insurgent*, nos. 4/5 (Spring 1979), p. 14-15; *Librarians for social change*, no. 21 (Winter 1979), p. 21; "Out of the closet and into the catalog: access to Gay/Lesbian library materials," *Interracial books for children bulletin*, v. 14, nos. 3/4 (1983), p. 31-2.
  Comments/citations: *Report of the Racism and Sexism in Subject Analysis Subcommittee to the RTSD/CCS Subject Analysis Committee, Midwinter 1980* (3d revision, June 1980), p. 13.

- Compiler, *We're UNREAL! A selection of subject headings in the Hennepin County Library catalog for fictional people, places and things* (Hennepin County Library, July 1978). 6-panel folded bookmark.

- Compiler, "Index," in E.J. Josey, ed., *The information society: issues and answers* (Oryx Press, 1978), p. 123-33.

- Consultant/contributor to Bill Katz and Berry G. Richards, eds., *Magazines for libraries* (3d ed.; Bowker, 1978).

- "The automated catalog and the demise of the cataloging mystique; or, Here comes the catalog the people always wanted . . . maybe," in *Requiem for the card catalog: management issues in automated cataloging* (Greenwood Press, 1979), p. 65–70. Unedited version, with bibliography, published as "The cataloging mystique — and automation," *HCL cataloging bulletin*, no. 32 (Jan./Feb. 1978), p. 15–25.

- Contributor/subject index compiler, *Serials for libraries;* compiled by Joan K. Marshall (Neal/Schuman; ABC-Clio, 1979). "Subject index": p. 467–94.

- Compiler, "Index," in Don Roberts and Deirdre Boyle, editors, *Mediamobiles: views from the road* (ALA, 1979), p. 107–16.

- "Access to alternatives: new approaches in cataloging," in *Alternative materials in libraries: a handbook* (Alternative Acquisitions Project, 1979), p. 33–63.
  Updated reprints: *Collection building*, v. 2, no. 2 (March 1980), p. 28–53; James P. Danky and Elliott Shore, eds., *Alternative materials in libraries* (Scarecrow Press, 1982), p. 31–66.
  Comments/citations: Eric J. Carpenter, "Small presses," in Patricia A. McClung, *Selection of library materials in the humanities, social sciences, and sciences* (ALA, 1985), p. 347; Patricia J. Case, "Antidote to the homogenized library," *New Pages*, no. 6 (Spring 1983), p. 7; Constance Rinehart, "Subject cataloging in 1982," *Library resources & technical services*, v. 27, no. 3 (July/Sept. 1983), p. 270, 275.

- "Cataloging for public libraries," in Maurice J. Freedman and S. Michael Malinconico, eds., *The nature and future of the catalog* (Oryx Press, 1979), p. 225–39.
  Comments/citations: Gregg Sapp, "Levels of access: subject approaches to fiction," *RQ*, v. 25, no. 4 (Summer 1986), p. 492, 496.

- "Proposed: AACR2 options and addenda for school and public libraries," *HCL cataloging bulletin*, no. 38 (Jan./Feb. 1979), p. 24–6.
  Comments/ciations: "Selected bibliography on AACR2," in *The making of a code: the issues underlying AACR2* (A.L.A., 1980), p. 235–6.

- "Proposed: a subject cataloging code for public and school libraries," *HCL cataloging bulletin*, no. 39 (March/April 1979), p. 1–5.
  Updated reprint: "A subject cataloging code for public, school, and community college libraries — a proposal," *Unabashed librarian*, no. 32 (1979), p. 19–20.
  Comments/citations: William E. Studwell, "Why not an 'AACR' for subject headings?," *Cataloging & classification quarterly*, v. 6, no. 1 (Fall 1985), p. 5, 8.

- Compiler, "Index," in Maurice J. Freedman and S. Michael Malinconico, eds., *The nature and future of the catalog* (Oryx Press, 1979), p. 291–317.

- "1. Libraries — Forecasts. 2. Elitism in librarianship," *Library journal*, v. 105, no. 1 (Jan. 1, 1980), p. 23–7.
  Comments/citations: "Letters," *Library journal*, April 15, 1980, p. 891; Peter Gellatly, "The Eighties: editorial," *Serials librarian*, v. 5, no. 1 (Fall 1980), p. 4; Susan L. Heath, "Intellectual freedom: one answer for the 1980s in Wisconsin," *Wisconsin library bulletin*, v. 77, no. 1 (Spring 1981), p. 36.

- Compiler, "Index," In Marian S. Edsall, *Library promotion handbook* (Oryx Press, 1980), p. 232–44.

- Compiler, "Index," in *Networks for networkers: critical issues in cooperative library development* (Neal-Schuman, 1980), p. 419–44.

- "Cataloging Castaneda," in Richard de Mille, ed., *The Don Juan papers: further*

*Castaneda controversies* (Ross-Erikson Publishers, 1980), p. 100–3.
  Comments/citations: Jane L.C. Gosney, *Library journal,* April 15, 1980, p. 982.

- Compiler, "Index," in E.J. Josey, ed., *Libraries in the political process* (Oryx Press, 1980), p. 299–322.

- "DDC 19: an indictment," *Library journal,* v. 105, no. 5 (March 1, 1980), p. 585–89.
  Comments/citations: "Letters," *Library journal,* June 1, 1980, p. 1240; "Letters," *Library journal,* June 15, 1980, p. 1339; "Letters," *Library journal,* July 1980, p. 1444; "Letters," *Library journal,* August 1980, p. 1555–6; Elizabeth M. Dickinson, "Dewey Decimal Classification, Edition 19: schedules relating to men, women, age levels, and alternative relationships," in *Report of the Racism and Sexism in Subject Analysis Subcommittee to the RTSD/CCS Subject Analysis Committee, Midwinter 1980* (3d revision, June 1980), Appendix 3, p. 1; Elizabeth Dickinson, "Living with DDC 19," *Technicalities,* v. 1, no. 13 (Dec. 1981), p. 10–11; Hans W. Wellisch, "Year's work in subject analysis: 1980," *Library resources & technical services,* July/Sept. 1981, p. 297; Richard A. Gray, "Disasters: natural, nuclear, and classificatory," *RQ,* v. 22, no. 1 (Fall 1982), p. 42, 47; Richard A. Gray, "Classification schemes as cognitive maps," *Reference librarian,* no. 9 (Fall/Winter 1983), p. 146, 153; John A. Humphrey and Judith Kramer-Greene, "DDC and its users: current policies," *ibid.,* p. 155, 163; Arthur Curley and Jana Varlejs, *Akers' simple library cataloging* (Scarecrow Press, 1984), p. 169–70.
  Reprint: Bill Katz, ed., *Library lit. 11 — the best of 1980* (Scarecrow Press, 1981), p. 99–107.

- Compiler, "Subject index," in Maureen Crowley, ed., *Energy: sources of print and nonprint materials* (Neal-Schuman, 1980), p. 327–41.

- "If there were a *Sex index* . . .," in Peter Gellatly, ed., *Sex magazines in the library collection: a scholarly study of sex in serials and periodicals* (Haworth Press, 1980), p. 99–135.
  Comments/citations: Eric Moon, "Sex mags study," *Library journal,* July 1980, p. 1492; Eli Oboler, *Newsletter on intellectual freedom,* Sept. 1981, p. 122; Mark Rabnett, *Manitoba Library Association Bulletin,* v. 12, no. 4 (Sept. 1982), p. 24; Gregg Sapp, "Levels of access: subject approaches to fiction," *RQ,* v. 25, no. 4 (Summer 1986), p. 494, 497.

- "Living amid closed catalogs," in D. Kaye Gapen and Bonnie Juergen, eds., *Closing the catalog: proceedings of the 1978 and 1979 Library and Information Technology Association Institutes* (Oryx Press, 1980), p. 147–51.
  Reprint: Cynthia C. Ryans, ed., *The card catalog: current issues; readings and selected bibliography* (Scarecrow Press, 1981), p. 89–93.
  Comments/citations: James R. Dwyer, "The effect of closed access on public access," *Library resources & technical services,* v. 25, no. 2 (April/June 1981), p. 194–5.

- Compiler, "Index," in D. Kaye Gapen and Bonnie Juergens, eds., *Closing the catalog* (Oryx Press, 1980), p. 177–94.

- Compiler, "Index," in Carol H. and James L. Thomas, eds., *Meeting the needs of the handicapped: a resource for teachers and librarians* (Oryx Press, 1980), p. 439–79.

- "Title access," *Technicalities,* v. 1, no. 1 (Dec. 1980), p. 6–7.
  Comments/citations: Janet Swan Hill, "Letters to the editor," *Technicalities,* v. 1, no. 2 (Jan. 1981), p. 2; retort: v. 1, no. 4 (March 1981), p. 2.

- "Space Age hardware, Stone Age data," *SRRT newsletter,* #57 (Sept. 1980), p. 3.

- Compiler, "Index," in *Using AACR2: a diagrammatic approach* (Oryx Press, 1981), p. 181-99.

    Comments/citations: Mary Dykstra, "Algorithms & 'AACR 2,'" *Library journal,* Oct. 15, 1981, p. 2001; Jeanne Osborn, *American reference books annual* (1982), p. 143-4.

- *Joy of cataloging: essays, letters, reviews, and other explosions* (Oryx Press, 1981), 249 p.

    Reviews: Frank Bright, *Added entries* (Memorial Library, University of Wisconsin-Madison), no. 173 (June 5, 1981), p. 5-6; Noel Peattie, *Sipapu,* v. 12, no. 1 (1981), p. 12-13; Sophie K. Black, *Booklist,* Oct. 15, 1981, p. 283; Susan Traill, *Emergency librarian,* Sept./Oct. 1981, p. 19-20; Anita Garey, *WLWjournal,* April/Sept. 1981, p. 14-15; Tom Jedele, *PLAFSEP,* no. 17 (Winter 1981/82), p. 2-3; Jeanne Osborn, *American reference books annual* (1982), p. 136; Grant Burns, *New pages,* v. 2, no. 1 (Spring 1982), p. 17; Robert Lincoln, *Manitoba Library Association Bulletin,* v. 12, no. 3 (June 1982), p. 10-11; J.M. Perreault, "'A representative of the New Left in American subject cataloguing': a review essay on Sanford Berman's *The Joy of cataloging,*" in *Dialogue on the subject catalogue* (University of Illinois Graduate School of Library and Information Science, 1983; Occasional papers, no. 161), p. 3-29; *American notes & queries,* Sept./Oct. 1983.

    Comments/citations: *Resources in library and information science* (OPLIC, St. Paul), #30 (April/May 1981), p. 3; *Recent publications on governmental problems* (Merriam Center Library, Chicago), v. 50, no. 10 (May 15, 1981), p. 5; *Consumer health info* (Twin Cities Biomedical Consortium), v. 4, no. 12 (Dec. 1981), p. 5; "Bibliography," *Maledicta,* v. 5, nos. 1/2 (Summer/Winter 1981), p. 328; Gail J. Junion, "Guide to reference tools for cataloging Africana," *Library resources & technical services,* v. 26, no. 2 (April/June 1982), p. 121; Dick DeBacher, "The Oryx Press: information, high-technology, and libraries," *Library and information science annual* (1987), p. 17; Jennifer A. Younger, "Year's work in subject analysis: 1981," *Library resources & technical services,* July/Sept. 1982, p. 267, 272; James C. Thompson and Kay A. Flowers, "Pseudoscience, creationism and the library," *Catholic library world,* 1984, p. 178-9; Lois M. Pausch and Robert H. Burger, "Making of the adaptable cataloger," *Illinois libraries,* v. 67, no. 5 (May 1985), p. 441-2; Russell Ash and Brian Lake, *Bizarre books* (Macmillan London, 1985), p. 130; Gregg Sapp, "Levels of access: subject approaches to fiction," *RQ,* v. 25, no. 4 (Summer 1986), p. 492, 497.

    Reprint: "From sea to shining sea . . . to Inland sea . . . to Sea combined with rudder . . . to Sea for the inland boatman . . . to Sea, inland edition," in Susan M. Murray, editor, *Toronto Health Libraries Association Union list of periodicals* (4th ed.: 1984), p. 1-2.

- "LCSH: an exchange between Mary Kay Pietris and Sandy Berman," *Technicalities,* v. 1, no. 4 (March 1981), p. 5-7, 9.

- "The local library and the small press," *Small press review,* v. 13, no. 6 (June 1981), p. 37-8.

    Comments/citations: Cristine Rom, "Little magazines: do we really need them?," *Wilson library bulletin,* v. 56, no. 7 (March 1982), p. 517, 519; Eric J. Carpenter, "Small presses," in Patricia A. McClung, *Selection of library materials in the humanities, social sciences, and sciences* (ALA, 1985), p. 345; Trish Harper, "The public library and small presses: surviving, hopeful, and full of surprises," *Show-me libraries,* Oct./Nov. 1982, p. 9; Patricia J. Case, "Antidote to the homogenized library," *New pages,* no. 6 (Spring 1983), p. 7.

- "Berman on consumerism: a guest editorial," *Technicalities,* v. 1, no. 2 (Nov. 1981), p. 1.

    Reprint: *Librarians for social change,* v. 10, no. 1 (1982), p. 2.

- "Consumer, beware!," *Technicalities,* v. 1, no. 12 (Nov. 1981), p. 11–2; v. 1, no. 13, (Dec. 1981), p. 3, 11; v. 2, no. 1 (Jan. 1982), p. 6–7; v. 2, no. 2 (Feb. 1982), p. 6–7; v. 2, no. 3 (March 1982), p. 10–11; v. 2, no. 4 (April 1982), p. 9–10; v. 2, no. 5 (May 1982), p. 8–10; v. 2, no. 6 (June 1982), p. 8–9; v. 2, no. 7 (July 1982), p. 7, 16; v. 2, no. 8 (August 1982), p. 8–9; v. 2, no. 9 (September 1982), p. 3, 7; v. 2, no. 10 (October 1982), p. 11–13; v. 2, no. 11 (Nov. 1982), p. 11–12; v. 2, no. 12 (December 1982), p. 14–15; v. 3, no. 1 (Jan. 1983), p. 9–10; v. 3, no. 2 (Feb. 1983), p. 10–11; v. 3, no. 3 (March 1983), p. 6–7; v. 3, no. 4 (April 1983), p. 5–6; v. 3, no. 5 (May 1983), p. 3–5, 8; v. 3, no. 6 (June 1983), p. 15–16; v. 3, no. 7 (July 1983), p. 2, 12; v. 3, no. 8 (August 1983), p. 15–16; v. 3, no. 10 (October 1983), p. 2, 12; v. 3, no. 12 (Dec. 1983), p. 10–11, 15; v. 4, no. 2 (Feb. 1984), p. 5–6, 10; v. 4, no. 3 (March 1984), p. 5–6, 16; v. 4, no. 6 (June 1984), p. 10–11; v. 4, no. 10 (October 1984), p. 11–13; v. 4, no. 12 (Dec. 1984), p. 8–10; v. 5, no. 2 (Feb. 1985), p. 6–8; v. 5, no. 4 (April 1985), p. 8–9; v. 5, no. 6 (June 1985), p. 13–15; v. 5, no. 8 (August 1985), p. 7–9, 15; v. 5, no. 10 (October 1985), p. 13–15; v. 5, no. 12 (Dec. 1985), p. 9–11; v. 6, no. 2 (Feb. 1986), p. 12–13, 15; v. 6, no. 5 (May 1986), p. 14–15; v. 6, no. 6 (June 1986), p. 3–4; v. 6, no. 8 (August 1986), p. 9–10; v. 6, no. 11 (Nov. 1986), p. 13–15; v. 6, no. 12 (Dec. 1986), p. 8–11; v. 7, no. 1 (Jan. 1987), p. 12–13; v. 7, no. 3 (March 1987), p. 10–11; v. 7, no. 4 (April 1987), p. 11–12; v. 7, no. 5 (May 1987), p. 5–7; v. 7, no. 6 (June 1987), p. 12, 14.

- "'Inside' censorship," *Wisconsin library bulletin,* v. 77, no. 1 (Spring 1981), p. 21–4.

  Abridged reprints: *North country anvil,* #40 (Aug./Sept. 1982), p. 20–2; *Librarians for social change,* v. 10, no. 2 (1982), p. 3–6.

  Comments/citations: Patricia J. Case, "Antidote to the homogenized library," *New pages,* no. 6 (Spring 1983), p. 7; Lester Asheim, "Selection and censorship: a reappraisal," *Wilson library bulletin,* Nov. 1983, p. 184.

- "Reference, readers and fiction: new approaches," *Reference librarian,* nos. 1/2 (Fall/Winter 1981), p. 45–53.

  Comments/citations: Audrey Taylor, *PRECIS indexing in school libraries: a tool for tomorrow today* (paper presented at International Association of School Librarianship Annual Conference, August 1–6, 1982, Red Deer, Alberta, Canada), p. 11; Gregg Sapp, "Levels of access: subject approaches to fiction," *RQ,* v. 25, no. 4 (Summer 1986), p. 492–3, 497.

- Compiler, "Index," in James P. Danky and Elliott Shore, editors, *Alternative materials in libraries* (Metuchen, NJ: Scarecrow Press, 1982), p. 211–45.

- Compiler, *Technicalities: index to volume 1* (Oryx Press, 1982), 12 pages.

- "Do-it-yourself subject cataloging," *Library journal,* v. 107, no. 8 (April 15, 1982), p. 785–6.

  Comments/citations: Constance Rinehart, "Subject cataloging in 1982," *Library resources & technical services,* v. 27, no. 3 (July/Sept. 1983), p. 270, 275; American Library Association Ad Hoc Subcommittee on Subject Access to Microcomputer Software, *Guidelines on subject access to microcomputer software* (1986), p. 22.

- Consultant/indexer, *Alternative papers: selections from the alternative press, 1979–1980* (Philadelphia: Temple University Press, 1982). "Index": p. 487–521.

  Index comments/citations: *American libraries,* Sept. 1982, p. 551; Kenneth F. Kister, *Library journal,* Oct. 1, 1982, p. 1875; Bill Katz, *Library journal,* Dec. 15, 1982, p. 2324; Neal Edgar, *Newsletter on intellectual freedom,* Jan. 1983, p. 6; Grant Burns, *New pages,* no. 6 (Spring 1983), p. 9.

- "'The Jewish Question' in library cataloging," *Shmate,* v. 1, no. 3 (Sept./Oct. 1982), p. 8–12. Revised and updated version of the 1979 AJL Convention paper originally published as "The 'Jewish Question' in Subject Cataloging," in *Joy of cataloging* (1981), p. 113–23.
  Comments/citations: "Library followup," *Shmate,* v. 1, no. 4 (Jan. 1983), p. 3, 23.

- Compiler, "Subject index," in Renee Feinberg, *Women, education, and employment: a bibliography of periodical citations, pamphlets, newspapers and government documents, 1970–1980* (Library Professional Publications, 1982), p. 247–74.
  Comments/citations: Donna L. Nerboso, *Library Journal,* Dec. 15, 1982, p. 2330; Donna L. Nerboso, "Studying 'the 80%': a selected guide to bibliographic sources on working women," *Behavioral and social sciences librarian,* Spring 1985, p. 67.

- Compiler, *Technicalities: index to volume 2* (Oryx Press, 1983). 16 pages.

- Compiler, "Subject index," *Information America,* v. 6, no. 1 (1983), p. 147–61; v. 6, no. 2 (1983), p. 163–90; v. 6, no. 3 (1983), p. 148–88; v. 7, no. 1 (1984), p. 141–57; v. 7, no. 2 (1984), p. 144–76; v. 7, no. 3 (1985), p. 138–81.

- "Good information," *North Country Anvil,* no. 45 (Fall 1983), p. 9–10.

- Contributor, *A dialogue on the subject catalogue* (University of Illinois Graduate School of Library and Information Science, 1983; Occasional papers, no. 161), p. 30–44, 54–6, 59–60.

- "Predictions," *Technical services quarterly,* v. 1, nos. 1/2 (Fall/Winter, 1983), p. 61–3.
  Reprinted excerpt: "An 'automation gap,'" *Library administrator's digest,* v. 19, no. 8 (Oct. 1984), p. 58.
  Comments/citations: Richard L. Waters, *Public Library Quarterly,* v. 6, no. 1 (Spring 1985), p. 104; Jeanne Osborn, *Library science annual,* v. 1 (1985), p. 144.

- Compiler, *Technicalities: index to volume 3* (Oryx Press, 1984). 19 pages.

- "Where have all the Moonies gone?," *Reference librarian,* no. 9 (Fall/Winter 1983), p. 133–43.
  Reprinted excerpt: *American libraries,* April 1984, p. 227.
  Comments/citations: Janice Shea, *Canadian library journal,* Oct. 1984, p. 304.

- "Action-recommendations to PLA Cataloging Needs Committee," *Unabashed librarian,* no. 48 (1983), p. 13–14.

- Co-editor/indexer, *Alternative library literature, 1982/1983: a biennial anthology* (Oryx Press, 1984). 338 p.
  Reviews: Grant Burns, *New Pages,* no. 8 (Fall 1984), p. 19; *Workbook,* v. 9, no. 4 (Oct./Dec. 1984), p. 157–8; Jim Dwyer, *Library Journal,* Dec. 1984, p. 2246; Norman Stevens, *Wilson library bulletin,* Nov. 1984; *Booklist,* Jan. 15, 1985, p. 683; Noel Peattie, *Sipapu,* v. 15, no. 2 (1984), p. 15–16; Kay Cassell, *Voice of Youth Advocates,* v. 7, no. 6 (Feb. 1985), p. 352; Leslie Kahn, *Women in libraries,* March/April 1985, p. 7; Jackie Eubanks, *Interracial books for children bulletin,* v. 16, nos. 2/3 (1985), p. 28; Cristine C. Rom, *Serials review,* Spring 1985, p. 44–5; Jennifer Lodde, *WLA* [Wisconsin Library Association] *journal,* no. 1 (June 1985), p. 79–80; Joseph W. Palmer, *Library science annual,* v. 1 (1985), p. 109; Kathleen Hirooka, *WLW journal,* v. 10 (1985), p. 8.
  Comments/citations: *Whole again resource guide, 1986/87,* p. 53.

- "Nukes in the library: an antidote to media suppression," *New pages,* no. 8 (Fall 1984), p. 17–18.

- Editor/contributor/indexer, *Subject cataloging: critiques and innovations* (Haworth Press, 1984). 252 pages. Also issued as *Technical services quarterly*, v. 2, nos. 1/2 (Fall/Winter 1984).

  Reviews: Peter Lisbon, *American libraries*, April 1985, p. 228, 248; *Booklist*, April 15, 1985, p. 1158; Norman Stevens, *Wilson library bulletin*, May 1985, p. 618–19; Jeanne Osborn, *Library science annual*, v. 1 (1985), p. 81; Jean Martin Perreault, *International classification*, v. 12, no. 3 (1985); Doris Hargrett Clack, *Journal of education for library and information science*, Spring 1986.

  Comments/citations: Sheila S. Intner, "Recent technical services research: an analysis," *RTSD newsletter*, v. 11, no. 2 (1986), p. 10–11; Pauline A. Cochrane, *Improving LCSH for use in online catalogs* (Libraries Unlimited, 1986), p. 4, 8; Doris Cruger Dale and Betty-Ruth Wilson, "Survey of the literature on subject analyis for 1984–1985," *Library resources & technical services*, July/Sept. 1986, p. 274–7, 280–1, 283; Candy Schwartz/Laura Malin Eisenmann, "Subject analysis," in *Annual review of information science and technology* (1986), p. 43, 51.

- "Proposal for reforms to improve subject searching," *American Libraries*, April 1984, p. 254.

  Comments/citations: Pauline A. Cochrane, *Improving LCSH for use in online catalogs* (Libraries Unlimited, 1986), p. 43.

  Reprint: Cochrane, p. 121–2.

- "In the beginning: Creationism and the schools," *Shmate*, nos. 11/12 (Summer 1985), p. 44–6.

  Comments/citations: Noel Peattie, "Our reaction...," *Sipapu*, no. 35 (1985), p. 19.

- "Genesis caper," *Utne reader*, no. 10 (June/July 1985), p. 16–17.

  Reprint: *Minnesota Skeptics newsletter*, Jan. 1986, p. 2.

- Editor, "The censorship scene: Minnesota Reviews supplement," *Minnesota reviews*, Aug./Sept. 1985, p. S9–16.

- "'Give peace a chance': subject access to material on nukes, militarism, and war," *Technical services quarterly*, v. 3, nos. 1/2 (Fall 1985/Winter 1985/86), p. 113–26.

  Comments/citations: "Berman's new 'nuke' subject headings," *LNAC almanac*, Fall/Winter 1986, p. 3; Paul G. Weiss, *Technical services quarterly*, v. 4, no. 2 (Winter 1986), p. 3 (retort: p. 3–6).

- "'In the beginning': the creationist agenda," *Library journal*, October 15, 1985, p. 31–4.

  Comments/citations: "Damming that old time religion: educational backlash against Creationist flood," *New pages*, no. 10 (Winter/Spring 1986), p. 4; John H. Rush, "Separating church & state," *Library journal*, Jan. 1986, p. 8; Charlotte M. Gunther, "Two separate areas of study," *ibid.*, p. 10; Joseph McDonald, "Bluster and threats," *Library journal*, Feb. 1, 1986, p. 8, 10; George A. Mindeman, "Devastating exposes," *ibid.*, p. 10; Beth M. Stenberg, "Teach your children well," *ibid.*, p. 10; Dennis Ingolfsland, "Support and suppression," *ibid.*, p. 12; "Library issues: a push for creationist books in libraries," *Creation/evolution newsletter*, Nov./Dec. 1985, p. 21; John Elliott, "Steve Martin, move over," *Library journal*, March 15, 1986, p. 7; "Articles of note," *Skeptical inquirer*, Spring 1986, p. 282; George Rickerson, "Correction & commendation," *Library journal*, April 1, 1986, p. 8; Timothy Perper, "Science through classification," *LJ*, May 1, 1986, p. 6; Ralph Nielsen, "Pseudoscience of Creationism," *ibid.*; Noel Peattie, *Sipapu*, v. 17, no. 1 (Spring 1986), p. 30–2; Ernie Lazar, *Creation/evolution bibliography/directory* (1987), p. 123.

  Retorts: "Religion and/or science," *Library journal*, March 15, 1986, p. 6–7.

- "Foreword," in David F. Kohn, *Cataloging and catalogs: a handbook for library management* (ABC-Clio, 1986), p. xiii–xiv.

  Comments/citations: Virgil L.P. Blake, *Library journal*, April 15, 1986, p. 62; Sheila S. Intner, "Library research," *RTSD newsletter*, v. 11, no. 8 (1986), p. 90.

  Abridged reprint: "Cataloging and catalogs," *Library administrator's digest*, v. 21, no. 3 (March 1986), p. 19.

- Editor/indexer, *Cataloging special materials: critiques and innovations* (Oryx Press, 1986). 198 pages.

  Reviews: Norman Stevens, *Wilson library bulletin*, Oct. 1986, p. 58–9; Helena M. Van Deroef, *Library journal*, Nov. 1, 1986, p. 50; Thomas Lehman, *RTSD newsletter*, v. 11, no. 7 (1986), p. 83; *Booklist*, Jan. 1, 1987, p. 681; JoAnn V. Rogers, *Library and information science annual* (1987), p. 86; *Reviewing librarian*, v. 12, no. 2 (1987), p. 78; *Sublines*, v. 4, no. 1 (1987); Marilyn Kogon, *Emergency librarian*, March/April 1987.

  Comments/citations: *Music cataloging bulletin*, v. 17, no. 12 (1986), p. 8; Sheila S. Intner, "Library research," *RTSD newsletter*, v. 11, no. 8 (1986), p. 90–1.

- Co-author, "Amandla! Attack on Apartheid," *New pages*, no. 11 (Fall 1986), p. 1, 9–13.

  Comments/citations: *Africana libraries newsletter*, no. 48 (Dec. 1986), p. 4.

- "Alternative perspectives: a conversation with Sandy Berman," *Technicalities*, v. 6, no. 10 (Oct. 1986), p. 3–9.

  Comments/citations: *SRRT newsletter*, no. 84 (June 1987), p. 3, 5.

- Co-editor/contributor/indexer, *Alternative library literature, 1984/1985: a biennial anthology* (McFarland, 1986). 247 pages.

  Reviews: John Crawford, *ASPC newsletter*, v. 1, no. 1 (Jan./Feb. 1987), p. 9; *Workbook*, v. 12, no. 1 (Jan./March 1987), p. 26–7; *Booklist*, April 1, 1987, p. 1175; Meta Nissley, *Technicalities*, March 1987, p. 12; Noel Peattie, *Sipapu*, v. 17, no. 2 (Late 1986), p. 21; Leonard Kniffel, *New pages*, no. 12 (Spring/Summer 1987), p. 7–8; Jim Dwyer, *Library journal*, May 15, 1987, p. 56; Norman Stevens, *Wilson library bulletin*, May 1987, p. 59; Jeanne Kocsis, *SRRT newsletter*, no. 84 (June 1987), p. 7; Joseph W. Palmer, *Library and information science annual* (1987), p. 62; Wallace White, *Newsletter on intellectual freedom*, July 1987, p. 124.

- "Terrible truth about teenlit cataloging," *Top of the news*, v. 43, no. 3 (Spring 1987), p. 311–20.

- Additional articles, poetry, letters, editorials, and reviews contributed to

  *Phylon, African affairs, Newsletter on intellectual freedom, African report, Junior natural history magazine, Quixote, Library journal, Journal of Negro history, Amnesty action, ALA bulletin, Los Angeles free press, Wilson library bulletin, UZ* (UNZA student newspaper), *University* (UNZA magazine), *Assistant librarian, Times literary supplement, Jewel of Africa, Mphala newsletter, Canadian library journal, Zambia Library Association Journal, Sipapu, School library journal, Library resources & technical services, Africana library journal, African studies review, Unabashed librarian, WorkForce, Syngergy, North Country librarian, American libraries, Rote Blaetter, Africana libraries newsletter, Jewish Librarians Caucus newsletter, Interracial books for children bulletin, Yin times of Black Bart, Twin Cities courier, College & research libraries, Administrator's digest, RQ, PLAFSEP, Public library quarterly, Voice of youth advocates, Humanist, Minnesota reviews, EMIE bulletin, Creation/evolution newsletter, LNAC almanac, Utne reader, Cultural survival quarterly, Northern sun, New Unionist, Minneapolis star & tribune.*

# INDEX